foreword

Yes, there is a change of mood in England: The mantra "Cool Britannia" is whispered loudly by the Government and the media. The Millennium Dome will show us, and the world, the best creative minds. The recent Powerhouse:UK exhibition forced foreign leaders to admire the best of British creative industry. 100% Design is the most exciting design event in the world. This is the best book of the best of British design. But let's not forget that publishing does not replace manufacturing, and exhibitions are no substitute for production. Let me spoil the party and say that there is hardly any design-led industry in England — definitely not enough to employ the hundreds of students churned out of design colleges every summer. The more self-congratulating the publication and the more smugly titled the event, the bigger the frustration, the bigger the compromise, the greater the mediocrity.

Milan is still the world capital of design, but it is no longer a closed shop. It is still the capital not for its designers but for its manufacturing culture and for its industry, which is committed to design.

In the early 1980s, France also experienced a change of mood; maybe the way they harnessed this mood had something to do with Milan opening its doors. Jacques Lang's Ministry of Culture set up an organization called VIA to promote French design by actually producing and marketing products of new designers. It made a lot of difference for young designers. One of the early beneficiaries of VIA was Phillipe Starck. More than anyone else, Starck signalled the invasion of "foreign" designers at the leading Italian design companies.

In the same period young British designers attracted attention for their crude, home-made designing/making. With no industry to work for, making was the only option — it came with its own aesthetics and charm. Towards the end of the decade, Italian manufacturers wanted to appropriate this exotic charm and started employing British designers, some of whom grasped the chance to design rather than make. There is now a noticeable number of British designers working for most of the important Italian firms — Cappellini, Moroso Driade, Kartell, Cassina, Alessi, Magis, Guzzini, and many more.

So, with new role models, new options, and new hopes, the ambitions of young British designers have begun to shift. Unfortunately, only a handful of them will be taken up by the Italians. It is clear that to make use of the celebrated young creative talent, the real change must come from the manufacturing industries in Britain.

Ron Arad

new british design 1998

general editor: peta levi

mitchell beazley

Dedication
To my loving husband Michael Sayers

First published in Great Britain in 1998 by
Mitchell Beazley, an imprint of Reed Consumer Books Limited
Michelin House, 81 Fulham Road, London SW3 6RB
also Auckland

Executive Editor: **Judith More**
Executive Art Editor: **Janis Utton**
Project Editor: **Julia North**
Production Controller: **Paul Hammond**

Produced for Mitchell Beazley by
The Design Revolution, Brighton
Designer: **Mark Roberts**
Editors: **Ian Whitelaw, Ian Kearey**

A CIP record for this book is available from the British Library.

ISBN 1 84000 099 6

The publishers have made every effort to ensure that all
information given in this book is accurate, but they can accept no
responsibility for any errors which may have occurred.

Typeset in Helvetica Neue

Colour origination by Radstock Reproductions Ltd, Britain

Printed and bound in Spain

contents

Introduction

In 1998 the UK has an international reputation for innovative design and craft. This is the result of a renaissance of design and craft skills, but this renaissance has not happened overnight — it has developed over the last 40 years. How has it come about? The reasons are complex, but because the phenomenon is the envy of people around the world I will try to explain how and why it developed.

First, there has been great development in design and craft education in the UK since the end of World War II, when there were only a handful of courses, mostly related to art and craft and not to design. Britain has made a major investment in its design education system. Around 62,000 students are currently enrolled on higher education art and design courses in the UK. Nearly 200 universities and colleges in Britain offer around 120 different subjects in art and design (source: Department of Education and Employment). The Netherlands Design Institute claims that the UK design education system produces around one-third of all Europe's design graduates.

Second, there has been a great stimulus from different cultures. Students come to the UK from all over the world to study. UK resident students come from a tremendous range of cultural and social backgrounds. They include the poor, the middle classes and the aristocracy. This helps to produce an extremely creative environment, rich with diverse ideas and influences.

Another major influence has been the Englishman's love of running a small business. Several waves of talented people have emerged from colleges at different times, triggering renewed interest in a particular area of craft or design. For example, in the 1950s a clutch of gifted silversmiths graduated from the Royal College of Art, including Gerald Benney, Robert Welch and David Mellor. These talented designers were leaving college and, unable either to get jobs with

Tom Dixon/Eurolounge
"Jack" by Tom Dixon. Multifunctional chair, modifiable for use as table base or light. Rotationally moulded polyethylene, various colourways.
60 x 60 x 60cm (23.5 x 23.5 x 23. 5in)
Eurolounge, 28 All Saints Road, London W11 1HG, England

British industry or to find manufacturers who would buy their designs, they resorted to making the products themselves. Gerald Benney developed a silversmithing workshop which at one time employed 22 people. He has probably made more silver for the Royal Family, for corporate patrons (including banks and religious bodies) and for private individuals worldwide than any other living craftsman. Robert Welch designs silver to commission and runs two shops, but he also designs for manufacture products which range from cooking utensils to lighting, glass and bathroom fittings. David Mellor has two shops, and he chose to start his own factory to manufacture his cutlery designs — some of the few to be manufactured in the UK today. These three spearheaded a new mood of optimism which ran through British art schools at the time, to take an "old" material such as silver and produce good, original British designs. Since that time colleges have been quick to latch onto new talent and to ask the newly-graduated "stars" to come back to college immediately after they graduate, in order to teach. As a result, a constant flow of fresh ideas and techniques is being taught to the next generation.

In the 1960s it was the turn of the furniture designers. Alan Peters, born in 1933 and the grandfather of the modern furniture movement, was apprenticed to Edward Barnsley – a direct link with the Arts and Crafts Movement which flourished at the turn of this century. Peters set up his own workshop in Devon in the early 1960s at the same time as John Makepeace started his workshop at Parnham in Dorset. At Parnham House Makepeace founded a school for furniture craftsmen in 1977. This has now taught over 220 students, most of whom have since set up their own businesses, designing and making furniture. With these two role models, a number of furniture designers emerged from the RCA in the late 1960s and 1970s. They included Fred Baier, David Field, Ashley Cartwright, Richard La Trobe Bateman and Rupert Williamson, all of whom set up their own workshops, designing and making furniture, usually one-off

Terence Woodgate/SCP Limited
Modular sofa system, solid beech frame, multi-density foam upholstery, silver powder-coated legs. Two- to four-seat sofas.
All configurations 69 x 85 x seat height 40cm (27 x 33.5 x 15.75in)
SCP Limited, 135-139 Curtain Road, London EC2A 3BX, England.

"THE NETHERLANDS DESIGN INSTITUTE CLAIMS THAT THE UK DESIGN SYSTEM PRODUCES AROUND ONE-THIRD OF ALL EUROPE'S DESIGN GRADUATES."

commissions. This established a trend for designers to set up their own workshops; that lifestyle was viewed as hard but satisfying, one that should at least enable the designer to survive. This trend may also have represented a protest against the silicon chip, comparable perhaps to William Morris's reaction against the ugliness and degraded standards to which the Industrial Revolution gave rise.

In 1971 the Crafts Council was set up, and it has subsequently given a great impetus to British crafts by encouraging them and setting standards of quality. The Council's setting-up grants, providing for maintenance and equipment, have enabled hundreds of designers to get started. Some of the Council's international conferences, such as those in 1976 on Studio Glass, in 1980 on Forging Iron, and in 1986 on Architectural Glass, have been of seminal importance, prompting a major burst of interest in developing contemporary studio and architectural glass and hand-forged metalwork.

In 1984, when I was Design Correspondent of House & Garden magazine, Condé Nast invited me to set up a scheme to try to bridge the gap between designers and industry. I spent the following eight years pioneering and developing the New Designers exhibition. This now brings together each July 2,000 of Britain's best graduating designers at the Business Design Centre in Islington, North London. One effect of having a national showcase for Britain's emerging young designers has been to turn graduates into much more commercial and hard-headed designers. Wanting their designs to be

generally accessible, they started batch-producing and mass-producing them.

In spite of these few initiatives, too many talented design graduates were trying to set up in business and were failing, largely through lack of support and advice. As a result, in 1994 I launched The Design Trust (TDT), a registered charity set up to promote the excellence of British design and craft, and to help with training once designers have left college, and its trading subsidiary, New Designers in Business Limited (NDB). Through NDB we have taken designers to over 40 international trade fairs over the last four years, and have helped them to market their products actively. NDB has helped over 300 young designers to establish successful businesses, not only by organising group stands at international trade fairs, thus helping to give them market credibility, but also by assisting with marketing and promotion; and TDT has provided business and technical training once designers have left college.

My vision for the future is to establish a Centre of Design Excellence in Central London, consisting of a retail outlet for the kinds of designs that you see in this book, an exhibition space for work by new designers, a public information resource centre and a training centre for young designers.

Today, where do you go to see or buy these contemporary British designs? Some London retail stores — among them the Conran Shop, Habitat, Heals, Harvey Nichols, Liberty, Selfridges and the newly established Haus in Mortimer Street, London — are starting to stock a few designs. There is a fast-growing number of specialist shops, and specialist galleries exist all over the UK. Many designers welcome visits by clients or prospective clients to their workshops, and many workshops hold regular open days — an example is Cockpit in Clerkenwell, London, with 150 designers and craftspeople.

In these pages you will gain insights into some of the interesting thought processes behind the designs, observe the interest in recycling materials and using everyday objects in design, discover the use of new technologies and see the fine craftsmanship which flourishes in all the design disciplines. This is an exciting time for British design. I hope that this book will give people around the world a glimpse of the diverse creativity to be found in the UK.

Peta Levi MBE

Jasper Morrison/SCP Limited
Desk top and drawer unit. Elm veneer, birch ply or embossed lacquer, stainless-steel legs, mild-steel base, aluminium drawer pulls.
75 x 100 x 200cm (29.5 x 39.5 x 78.75in)
SCP Limited, 135-139 Curtain Road, London EC2A 3BX, England.

01Ceramics

Introduction
Jane Priestman

To me, ceramics are the most overtly collectable of all the arts and crafts. From the earliest Chinese dynasties they have inspired generations of designers and collectors alike. The proverbial "passion for pots" has grown from an appreciation and delight in simple, practical utilities, through sophisticated urns and vases – archaic Greek and Egyptian, Roman and Japanese – to today, when the breadth, quality and choice of every type of ceramic are bewildering.

Every year we are inspired by the innovative and exciting developments pouring forth from colleges and universities. Experiments with every possible permutation and mix of materials and firings manifest themselves into a formidable array of ceramics. Stoneware, delicate china, precious metals, lustres and colours are becoming part of our everyday lives, from domestic utensils, such as Caterina Fadda's fresh concept of tableware (see page 21), to extraordinary dishes, bowls and vessels (see Stephen Dixon's teapot, page 18), garden pots and hand-moulded sculpture (see Virginia Dowe's figurative ceramics, page 19) – often in magical combinations.

In the last two decades, traditions established by time-honoured potters, such as Bernard Leach, Lucie Rie and Hans Coper, have been taken forward by a new generation of young designers – for example, Edmund de Waal, Abdo Nagi, Sue Mundy and Paul Priest – whose work you can see in this chapter and who have been quickly and sensibly picked up by the galleries.

"FROM THE SEDUCTIVE AND DELICATE TO THE EXPRESSIVE, LUSTY AND FORCEFUL, CERAMICS OF EVERY TYPE ARE A PLEASURE AND CONTINUE TO ENRICH OUR LIVES."

Architects, too, are beginning to realise that ceramics can become an integral part of their thinking when they want to enrich their buildings and urban developments. Increasing interest in the urban environment by the public has released possibilities for many designers; the unique austerity and presence of Jennifer Jones' enormous pots for exterior use can transform an open space into the tranquillity of a Japanese garden. One example of the successful use of ceramics in architecture is of the ceramic warriors designed by Peter Moss which adorn the conference rooms at the British Government's communications building at Vauxhall in London.

So, from the seductive and delicate to the expressive, lusty and forceful, ceramics of every type are a pleasure and continue to enrich our lives. Our young designers have not failed us – their fresh, innovative approach to this age-old craft can still stir feelings of immortality and touch our souls.

Detail from a vase by Antonia Salmon (see page 30)

01.01 **Antje Ernestus Ceramics**

Antje Ernestus
Foundry Hill Cottage
Corpusty Road
Wood Dalling
Norfolk NR11 6SD
England
Tel:+44 1263 587672

Education
BA (Hons) Ceramics,
Camberwell College of Art,
London, England, 1993

Collections/commissions
K. Lomp, private collection,
Neuwied, Germany,
1993–97
Commission for L. Ly,
London, England, 1996
Commissions for a German
architect and collector,
1995–97

Rectangular bowl
Terracotta and white stoneware clays, slab rolled, painted
with slips, cut, torn and textured.
33 x 40cm (13 x 15.75in)
To commission only

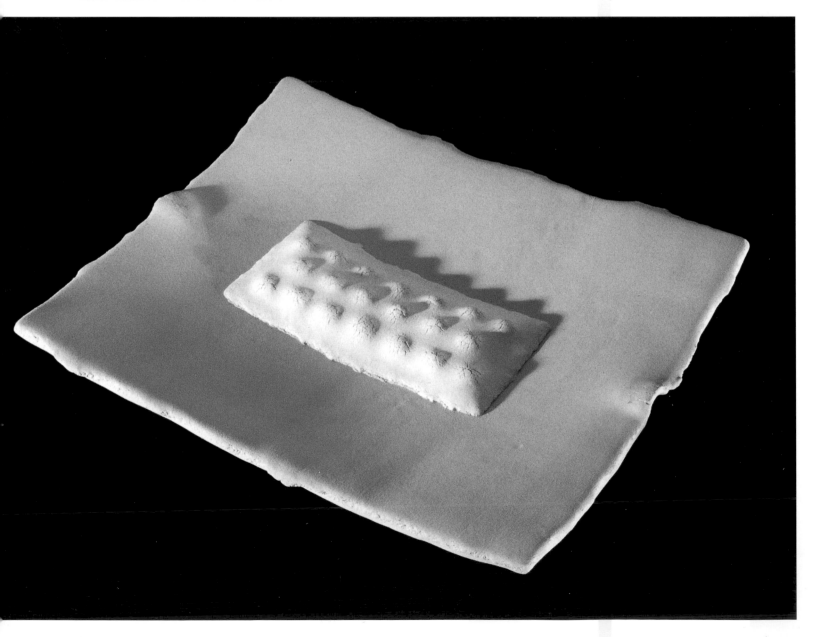

Jars and bowls
Two tall jars inlaid with copper and glazed in a Lucie Rie whiting glaze.
5.5 x 10.5cm (2.25 x 4in)
Large bowl inlaid with copper and glazed in a Derek Emms chun glaze.
15 x 6.5cm (6 x 2.5in)
Two medium bowls inlaid with copper, one with a whiting glaze, the other with a chun glaze.
11 x 6.5cm (4.25 x 2.5in)
All pieces to commission and through selected galleries

"THE UNCERTAINTY OF THE MEDIA, WORKING WITH PORCELAIN, AND THE INSTABILITY OF THE COMBINATION OF SUBTLE GLAZES WITH INLAID OXIDES ARE WHAT MAKES THE FINAL RESULT SO SPECIAL."

01.02 **Joanne Bergin**

Cedar House
25 Langham Road
Bowdon
Cheshire WA14 2HX
England
Tel:+44 161 941 7276
Fax:+44 161 941 7276

Education
BA (Hons) 3D Design,
Manchester Metropolitan
University, England, 1997

Collections/commissions
Commission, 48 pieces of
work for a New Zealand
gallery, 1998

01.03 **David Biddulph**

Standpoint Studios
45 Coronet Street
London N1 6HD
England
Tel:+44 171 729 5292
Fax:+44 171 729 3161

Education
BA (Hons) Workshop
Ceramics,
University of Westminster,
Harrow,
England, 1995

Platter
Stoneware, copper
red/black glaze,
reduction fired.
*11 x dia 27cm
(4.25 x 10.5in)*
To commission only

Two cup forms
Slab-built and smoke-fired with an application of terra
sigillata. 23ct gold leaf and 9ct gold wire,
polished with beeswax balsam.
Large – 8 x dia 7cm (3 x 2.75in)
Small – 6 x dia 6cm (2.5 x 2.5in)
To commission and through selected galleries

01.04	Joy Bosworth	22a Worcester Road

Hagley
near Stourbridge
West Midlands DY9 0LD
England
Tel:+44 1562 884810
Fax:+44 1562 884259

Education
BA (Hons) Art & Design,
Wolverhampton Polytechnic,
England, 1987
MA Art & Design Network,
University of Wolverhampton,
England, 1996

"A COLLECTION OF FOUND
ARTEFACTS FROM AN
INDUSTRIAL SOCIETY
INFORMS THE WORK.
BY USING 23CT GOLD LEAF I REFER
TO THE AMBIGUITIES IN THE
STATUS AND VALUE OF
THROWAWAY OBJECTS."

Ceramic vessels
Hand-built white stoneware clay. Porcelain and
bone china detail.
7 x 65cm (2.75 x 25.5in)
To commission only

01.05	Samantha Broady	33 Avondale Road

London N13 4DX
England
Tel:+44 181 886 8487

Education
BA (Hons) Ceramics,
Loughborough College of Art
& Design, England, 1997

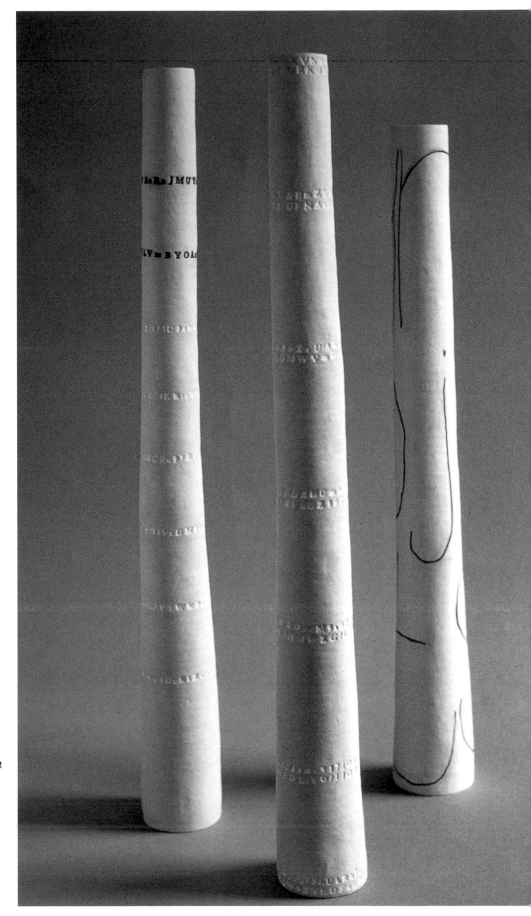

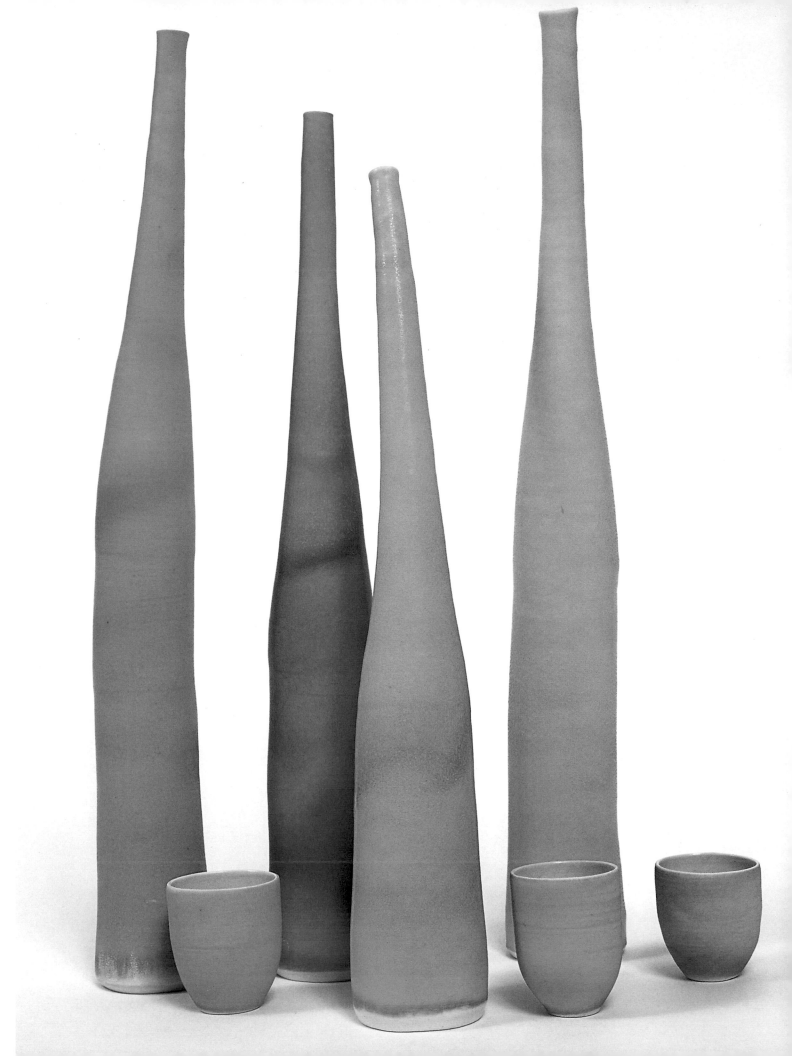

01.06 **Sophie Cook** 35a Hyde Vale
Greenwich
London SE10 8QQ
England
Tel: +44 181 692 7211
Fax: +44 181 692 7211

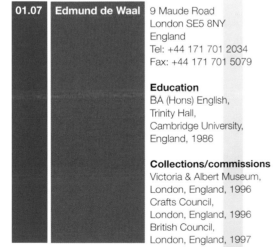

Education
BA Ceramics,
Camberwell College of Art,
London, England, 1997

Vases and beakers
Made from porcelain.
Thrown on the wheel.
Vases 50 x 10cm (19.5 x 4in)
Beakers 8 x 5cm (3.25 x 2in)
To commission only

Large lidded jar
Thrown using Limoges
porcelain, and finished
with a light celadon
glaze.
Height 45cm (17.75in)
To commission only

01.07 **Edmund de Waal** 9 Maude Road
London SE5 8NY
England
Tel: +44 171 701 2034
Fax: +44 171 701 5079

Education
BA (Hons) English,
Trinity Hall,
Cambridge University,
England, 1986

Collections/commissions
Victoria & Albert Museum,
London, England, 1996
Crafts Council,
London, England, 1996
British Council,
London, England, 1997

Teapot
"Diana." Hand-built vessel, decorated with coloured slips, glazes and lustres.
24 x 16 x 11cm (9.5 x 6.25 x 4.5in)
To commission only

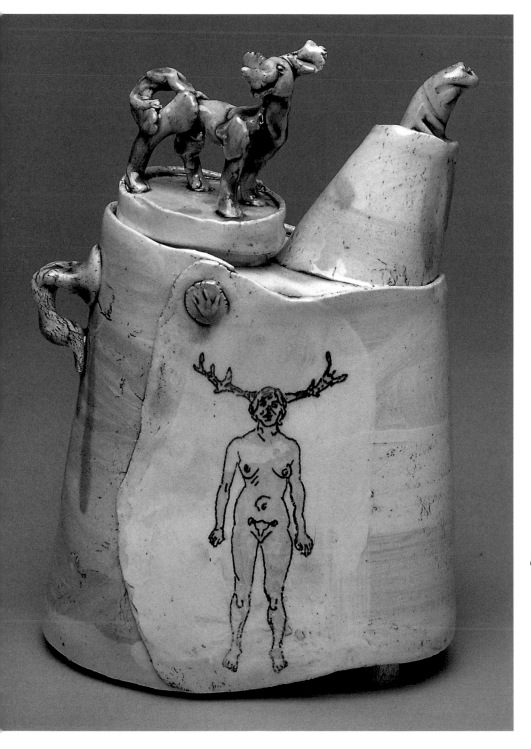

01.08   **Stephen Dixon**   21 Baldock Road
Didsbury
Manchester M20 6JG
England
Tel: +44 161 448 1540
Fax: +44 161 448 1540

Education
BA (Hons) Fine Art,
Newcastle University,
England, 1980
MA (RCA) Ceramics,
Royal College of Art,
London, England, 1986

Collections/commissions
"The Levantine Chess Set,"
Manchester City Art Gallery,
England, 1994
"More Tea Vicar" teapot,
Crafts Council,
London, England, 1997
"The Roast Beef of Old
England" teapot,
British Council,
London, England, 1997

"MY VESSELS CONTAIN OBLIQUE NARRATIVES, AN ATTEMPT TO COMBINE SOCIAL AND POLITICAL COMMENTARY WITH CONTEMPORARY DESIGN PRACTICE."

Figurative ceramics
"The Greeting." Ceramic (hand-building material),
high bisque, smoke-fired.
45 x 45 x 18cm (17.75 x 17.75 x 7in)
In production

01.09 | **Virginia Dowe** | 154 Henley Road
Ipswich, Suffolk IP1 4NS
England
Tel: +44 1473 286287

Education
BA (Hons)
3D Design (Ceramics),
University of Wolverhampton,
England, 1997

01.10 | **Emily Myers Ceramics**

Emily Myers
Alders Cottage
Crux Easton, near Newbury
Berkshire RG20 9QF
England
Tel: +44 1635 254435
Fax: +44 1635 254435

Education
BA (Hons) Ceramics,
Bristol Polytechnic, England,
1987

Collections/commissions
Aberystwyth Arts Centre,
permanent collection,
Wales, 1990
Stoke-on-Trent City Museum,
permanent collection,
England, 1993
Liverpool City Museum,
permanent collection,
England, 1997

Jar
Thrown in Keuper red clay.
Height 30cm (11.75in)
To commission only

"MY AIM IS TO PROPOSE
INNOVATIVE OBJECTS THAT
CHALLENGE THE PUBLIC PERCEPTION
OF FORM AND FUNCTION.
THIS WORK I DESCRIBE AS
DESIGN OBJECTS
WITH A CRAFT APPEAL."

01.11 | **Caterina Fadda** | E10 Peabody Estate
Dalgarno Gardens
London W10 5JH
England
Tel: +44 181 964 3725
Fax: +44 181 964 3725

Education
BA (Hons) Workshop
Ceramics,
University of Westminster,
Harrow, England, 1995
MA (RCA) Ceramics & Glass,
Royal College of Art,
London, England, 1997

Dinner sets
"Cellule." Slip-cast
earthenware,
dishwasher-safe.
Small bowl 13 x 10cm
(5 x 4in)
Large bowl 25 x 18cm
(9.75 x 7in)
Medium dish 37.5 x 27cm
(14.75 x 10.5in)
Large dish 40 x 30cm
(15.75 x 11.75in)
In production

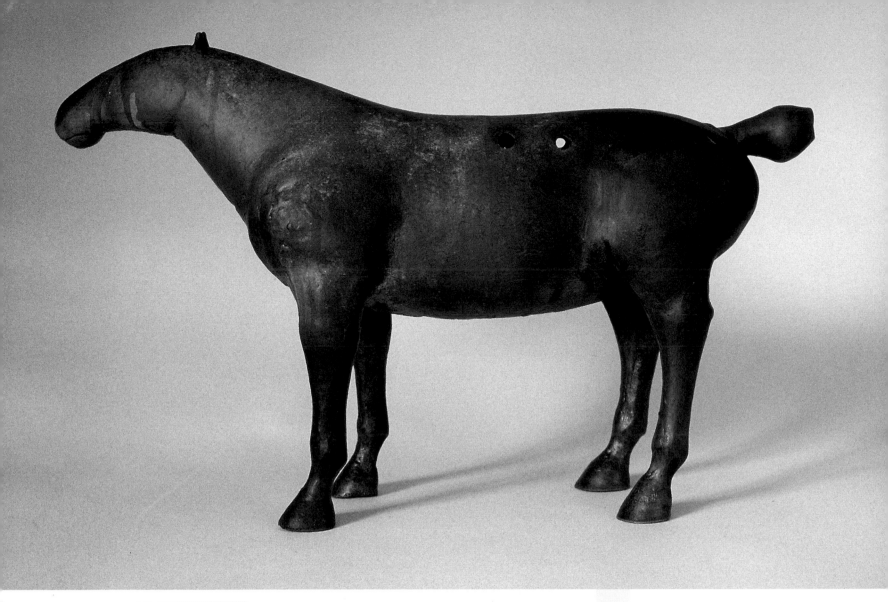

| 01.12 | Susan Halls | 198 Arbor Drive
Southport
CT 06490
USA
Tel: +1 203 254 9977
Fax: +1 203 254 9977

Sculpture
"Large Intelligent Horse." Paper clay, raku-fired with colloidal slips.
30 x 15 x 42cm (12 x 6 x 16.5in)
In production

Education
MA (RCA) Ceramics,
Royal College of Art,
London, England, 1990

Collections/commissions
Contemporary Art Society,
permanent collection,
London, England, 1994
Victoria & Albert Museum,
permanent collection,
London, England, 1993–97
Aberystwyth University,
permanent collection,
Wales, 1997

"I'M TRYING TO CREATE OBJECTS WHICH TRAP A KIND OF ANIMAL TRUTH, AN ICONIC SENSATION THAT DOES NOT RELY ON NARRATIVE OR HUMOUR."

01.13	Michael Sodeau Partnership	**Michael Sodeau and Lisa Giuliani**

Michael Sodeau and Lisa Giuliani
24 Rosebery Avenue
London EC1R 4SX
England
Tel: +44 171 837 2343
Fax: +44 171 837 2343

Education
Michael Sodeau — BA
(Hons) Product Design,
Central St Martins College
of Art & Design,
London, England, 1994

Vase
"Molar." In matt/satin white
slip-cast ceramic.
*27 x 20 x 11cm
(10.5 x 7.75 x 4.25in)
In production*

01.14 Sue Mundy

66 Highgrove Street
Reading
Berkshire RG1 5EN
England
Tel: +44 118 987 2956

Education
BA (Hons) Multi-Disciplinary
Design, North Staffordshire
University, England, 1986

Vessel
Made from T-material and
stoneware mixed. Coiled.
Texture by use of combs,
slips, latex, oxides. Glazed
inside. Reduction-fired.
20 x dia. 14cm
(7.75 x 5.5in)
To commission only

Slab bottles
Made from T-material and
white stoneware mixed.
Slab-built and reduction-
fired.
12-15 x 5cm (4.75-6 x 2in)
To commission only

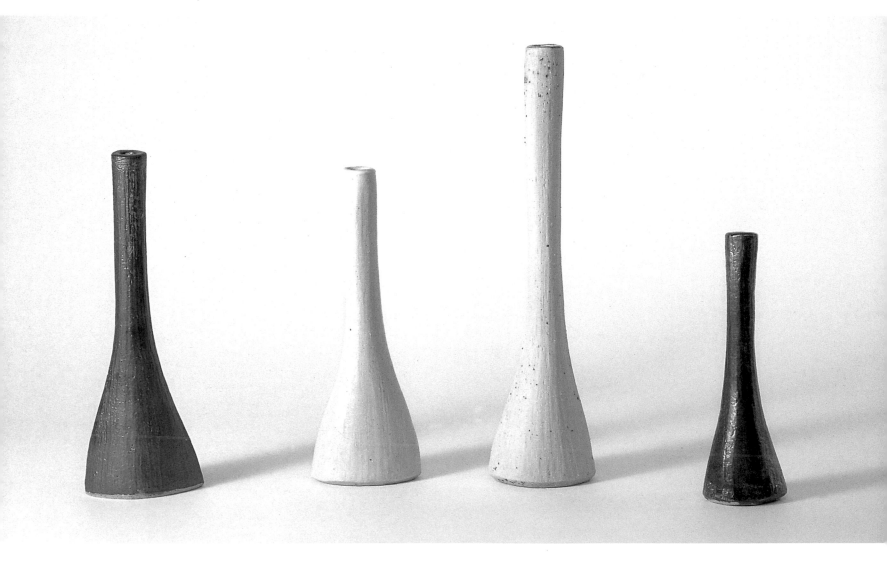

01.15 | **Abdo Nagi**

19 West View
Letchworth
Hertfordshire SG6 3QN
England
Tel: +44 1462 684461

Education
BA (Hons) Jewellery &
Ceramics,
Middlesex Polytechnic,
England, 1988

Collections/commissions
Carmarthen County Museum
(via Contemporary Art
Society), Wales, 1989
"Nature in Art,"
Wallsworth Hall,
Gloucestershire,
England, 1997
Letchworth Museum & Art
Gallery (via National Art
Collections Fund),
England, 1997

Pair of abstract vessels
"Surveillance." T-material
with various coloured slips.
Hand-built, coiling.
60 x 25cm (23.5 x 9.75in)
To commission only

"MY AIM IS ALWAYS TO
KEEP THE DESIGN
AS SIMPLE AS POSSIBLE,
GIVING OTHERS THE OPPORTUNITY TO
LET THEIR IMAGINATION
DO ITS WORK."

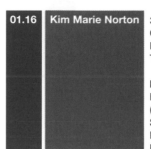

01.16 Kim Marie Norton

30 George Moore Close
Oxford OX4 4BZ
England
Tel: +44 1865 726415

Education
BA (Hons) 3D Design
(Ceramics),
Surrey Institute of Art &
Design, Farnham,
England, 1996

Structure
Slab-built, semi-porcelain
clay body with matt-white
lead glaze, coloured biscuit
slips and screen-printed
transfers.
33.5 x 18cm (13 x 7in)
To commission only

"I THROW PORCELAIN ON A STICK-DRIVEN MOMENTUM WHEEL, ALTER THE FORM AND HAND-CARVE EACH PIECE. THE PIECES ARE RAW-GLAZED IN CLASSICAL FINISHES AND FIRED IN A REDUCTION KILN. THESE ARE IMPORTANT TECHNIQUES TO ME, EMBRACING TRADITIONS AND THE HISTORY OF PORCELAIN, BUT IN THE 1990s."

Vessels
Small flared vessels in celadon, temoku and white. Thrown and altered on stick-driven momentum wheel. Hand-carved porcelain raw-glazed. Reduction-fired, creating elegant surface finishes.
10 x 22cm (4 x 8.5in)
To commission only

01.17 | **Sue Paraskeva**

70 Mountgrove Road
Highbury
London N5 2LT
England
Tel: +44 171 690 5131

Education
BA (Hons) 3D Design
(Ceramics),
Middlesex University,
England, 1995

Collections/commissions
24 individual pieces for a
Japanese wedding,
Niigata, Japan, 1996
94-piece dinner service for
Kevin Costner,
Los Angeles, USA, 1996-97

Ceramic sculpture
"Red Bull." Hand-built terracotta and glass-fibre 'sandwich'.
Raw-glazed and over-fired to a low stoneware. Rebuilt and
darkened in part to enhance. Mounted and signed on a
slate base.
85 x 15 x 44cm (34 x 6 x 17.5in)
In production

01.18 | **Paul Priest** | 71 Sunnycroft
Downley
High Wycombe
Buckinghamshire HP13 5UR
England
Tel:+44 1494 639 819
Fax:+44 1494 639 951

01.19   **Antonia Salmon**   20 Adelaide Road
Nether Edge
Sheffield
South Yorkshire S7 1SQ
England
Tel: +44 114 258 5971

Education
BA (Hons) Geography,
Sheffield University,
England, 1981
Diploma Studio Pottery,
Harrow School of Art,
England, 1984

Collections/commissions
Ismay private collection,
Wakefield, England, 1989
Sainsbury private collection,
London, England, 1992
Staffordshire Museum,
Stoke-on-Trent,
England, 1995

Sculpture
"Holding Piece." White stoneware, burnished and smoke-fired.
17 x dia. 16.5cm (6.75 x 6.5in)
In production

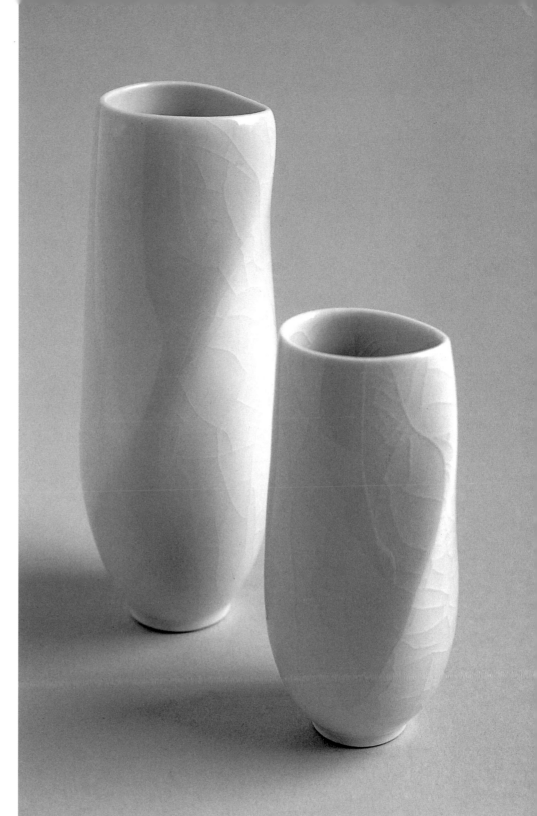

| 01.20 | Sarah-Jane Selwood | 15 North Fort Street
Leith, Edinburgh EH6 4HB
Scotland
Tel: +44 131 555 6075 |

Education
BA (Hons) Design,
Edinburgh College of Art,
Edinburgh, Scotland, 1991
Postgraduate Diploma
Design,
Edinburgh College of Art,
Edinburgh,
Scotland, 1992

Collections/commissions
Aberdeen Art Gallery,
permanent collection,
Scotland, 1996
Contemporary Ceramics,
permanent collection,
London, England, 1997–98

Vases
Pair of ice crackle vases. Porcelain wheel-thrown and distorted.
25 x 20cm (9.75 x 7.75in)
*To commission and work available from the Scottish Gallery,
Edinburgh, Scotland*

Teapots
Thrown porcelain, wisteria handles, dark brown semi-matt
and clear glazes.
21 x dia. 17cm (8.25 x 6.5in)
To commission only

01.21 **Julian Stair** 66 Milton Road
London SE24 0NP
England
Tel: +44 171 733 1007

Education
MA (RCA) Ceramics,
Royal College of Art,
London, England, 1981
PhD Critical Writing in
20th-Century British
Studio Ceramics,
Royal College of Art,
London, England, 1998

Collections/commissions
Victoria & Albert Museum,
permanent collection,
London, England, 1984
Sainsbury Centre for Visual
Arts, permanent collection,
Norwich, England, 1986
Boymans-van Beuningen
Museum, Rotterdam,
The Netherlands, 1996

Bodo Sperlein
145 de Beauvoir Road
London N1 4DL
England
Tel: +44 171 241 5204
Fax: +44 171 241 5202
E-mail: Lucysicks@aol.com

Education
BA (Hons) Ceramic Design,
Camberwell College of Art,
London, England, 1997

Collections/commissions
Plaster/bone china light
sculpture, Space,
London, England, 1997
Wall light installation,
Mission,
London, England, 1998

Tableware
Sculptural bone china, hand-textured and shaped tableware,
combines the modern and the classic.
Large plate dia. 35cm (13.5in) Small plate dia. 25cm (10in)
Large bowl dia. 25cm (10in) Small bowl dia. 13cm (5in)
In production

02**Glass**

Introduction
Peta Levi

The introduction of hot-blown studio glass into the UK at the end of the 1960s by the Mexican-born glass artist Sam Herman marked the beginning of a buoyant and lively period for UK glass designers. Colleges swiftly started courses to teach this new technique. For the first time, glass designers, released from the constraints of working with a team of skilled factory glass workers, were able to make beautiful, and sometimes way-out, glass on their own. Suddenly, after centuries of mainly utilitarian use, glass became a medium of fine art and a material in which to conceive and create, often directly, for purely aesthetic purposes.

Since the 1980s a reaction against the freedom of the hot-glass movement has taken place, and a shift has occurred towards learning glass-making skills from the old masters, in England, Venice and Sweden. However, the factory-produced glass from Eastern Europe was so good that it forced designers into pushing the art of glass-making further, to produce work that not only developed from a knowledge of the old skills but could be made solely by hand. One example of a designer who has gone through this process is Marianne H. Buus, who has just graduated from the Royal College of

Detail from a vase by Ruth Dresman (see page 53)

Art in London. She very much enjoys the process of making hot-blown glass, but has learnt it from old masters in Sweden. She has developed at the same time two strands of contrasting work. Influenced by painting and the use of colour, and aware of the transparency of glass, she creates rich layers of colour through which one can see. The three-dimensional nature of glass has also made her realise the importance of form, which has led to her "Trails" series of colourless frosted vessels (see page 42).

A number of glass designers are developing their own techniques. Emma O'Dare has developed an unusual *pâte-de-verre* technique, combining 75 percent recycled glass with 25 percent ceramic glaze ingredients to create a depth of colour and unusual texture not normally found in *pâte-de-verre* (see page 49).

Emily Jackson, who graduated from the University of Wolverhampton in 1997 and whose original interest was in ceramics, became inspired to work in glass after seeing the Crafts Council's exhibition "Contemporary British Glass" in 1993. Although influenced by glass artists such as Keiko Mukaide, Emily has developed her own technique of using cut glass canes, which she assembles in the form of a vessel using an optical adhesive, before kiln-fusing the piece using a sand-box technique (see page 48).

As each year passes, glass-making standards are rising. It is no longer sufficient to possess a good technique or to decorate surfaces — sensitivity towards the material is now the key to success. Glass designers also show an increasing tendency to produce practical as well as decorative objects. Bob Crooks of First Glass produces stemware and lighting as well as one-off pieces, and both Emma O'Dare and Emily Jackson are working towards using their techniques to produce lighting. At the same time, comments Bob Crooks, "there is a growing trend for people to collect one-off pieces of glass."

Since the Crafts Council's Studio Glass Conference in 1976 British glass artists have become less isolated and there has been increasing interaction within the international glass movement. This has resulted in a healthy interchange of ideas between glass artists around the world.

"IT IS NO LONGER SUFFICIENT TO POSSESS A GOOD TECHNIQUE OR TO DECORATE SURFACES — SENSITIVITY TOWARDS THE MATERIAL IS NOW THE KEY TO SUCCESS."

| 02.01 | Galia Amsel | 81 Callcott Road
London NW6 7EE
England
Tel: +44 181 357 2964
Fax: +44 181 357 2964 |

Education
BA (Hons) 3D Design,
Middlesex Polytechnic,
England, 1989
MA (RCA) Glass,
Royal College of Art,
London, England, 1991

Collections/commissions
Victoria & Albert Museum,
permanent collection,
London, England, 1994
Ulster Museum, permanent
collection, Belfast,
Northern Ireland, 1996
Tottenham Marshes Craft
Commission,
Lee Valley Regional Park,
London, England, 1997–98

Decorative piece
"Pierce 1." Lost-wax cast glass, sand-blasted and polished.
Coloured cone with copper.
25 x 7 x 80cm (10 x 2.75 x 31.5in)
To commission only

02.02 | Angela Berry Glass Design

Angela Berry
4 Callowend Cottages
Mappleton
Ashbourne
Derbyshire DE6 2AB
England
Tel: +44 1335 350448

Education
BA (Hons) Glass Design,
Staffordshire University,
England, 1997

Collections/commissions
Shipley Art Gallery,
permanent collection,
Gateshead,
England, 1998

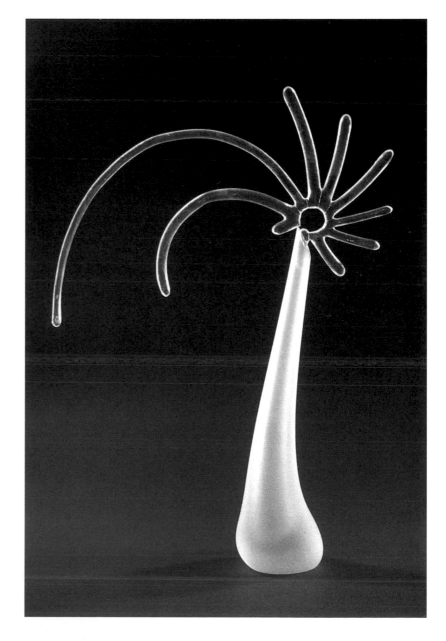

Perfume bottle
Free-blown bottle with hot-worked and kiln-formed stopper.
Bottle sand-blasted.
Height 20cm (8in)
In production

Vessel
"Water Drawing" series. Blown glass with applied decoration.
33 x 21 x 11cm (13 x 8.25 x 4.25in)
To commission only

| 02.03 | Phil Atrill | 26 Alcester Street |

Stoke
Plymouth
Devon PL2 1EF
England
Tel: +44 1752 500639

Education
BA (Hons) Design (Glass),
Edinburgh College of Art,
Scotland, 1995

Collections/commissions
Aberdeen City Arts Centre,
Scotland, 1996
National Trust for Scotland,
Gallery Shop,
The Hill House,
Helensburgh,
Scotland, 1998

02.04 | Belinda Hornsey Glass

Belinda Hornsey
11 Barry Avenue
Bucknall
Stoke-on-Trent
Staffordshire ST2 8AE
England
Tel: +44 1782 266197
Fax: +44 1782 266197

Education
BA (Hons) Glass,
Staffordshire University,
England, 1995

Collections/commissions
Ken Boddington,
Boddington Breweries,
Manchester, England, 1995
Lutz Borowski, FBG Anchor,
London, England, 1996
Dartington Crystal,
Devon, England, 1997–98

Vase
"Lotte." Form initially shaped with plaster. Two-part plaster mould then taken from form and molten glass blown into mould. When cold, cut, sand-blasted and polished.
27 x 10 x 12cm (10.5 x 4 x 4.75in)
In production

Glass dish
"Trails." Hand-formed glass, frosted.
8 x 26cm (3.25 x 10.25in)
To commission only

02.05	**Marianne H Buus**

8 Morgan Street
London E3 5AB
England
Tel: +44 181 980 0651
(Sweden: +45 86 222164)

Education
BA (Hons) Glass, Surrey
Institute of Art & Design,
Farnham, England, 1990
Apprentice, Transjö Hytta,
Kosta, Sweden, 1993-94
MA (RCA) Glass,
Royal College of Art,
London, England, 1997

Collections/commissions
Glass Museum, Ebeltoft,
Denmark, 1997
Commission for art trophy
for the 14th Annual Open
Exhibition,
Royal Overseas League,
London, England, 1997

Vase
Blown glass.
Height 31cm (12.5in)
To commission only

Will Shakspeare
Shakspeare Glassworks
Riverside Place
Taunton
Somerset TA1 1JJ
England
Tel: +44 1823 333422
Fax: +44 1823 333422
E-mail:
shakspeareglass@btint
or w.shakspeare@btinter
Website:
www.shakspeareglass.co.uk

Education
BA (Hons) 3D Design (Glass),
Surrey Institute of Art &
Design, Farnham,
England, 1983

"I AIM TO FIT FORM AND COLOUR TOGETHER, AND WHILST MOST OF MY WORK IS QUITE TIGHT IN FORM, THIS NEW RANGE IS KEPT DELIBERATELY LOOSE AND SIMPLE TO EXPRESS THE CONNECTION WITH THE INFLUENCES OF THE CULTURE AND ENVIRONMENTAL FACTORS OF MY EXPERIENCES IN CENTRAL AMERICA."

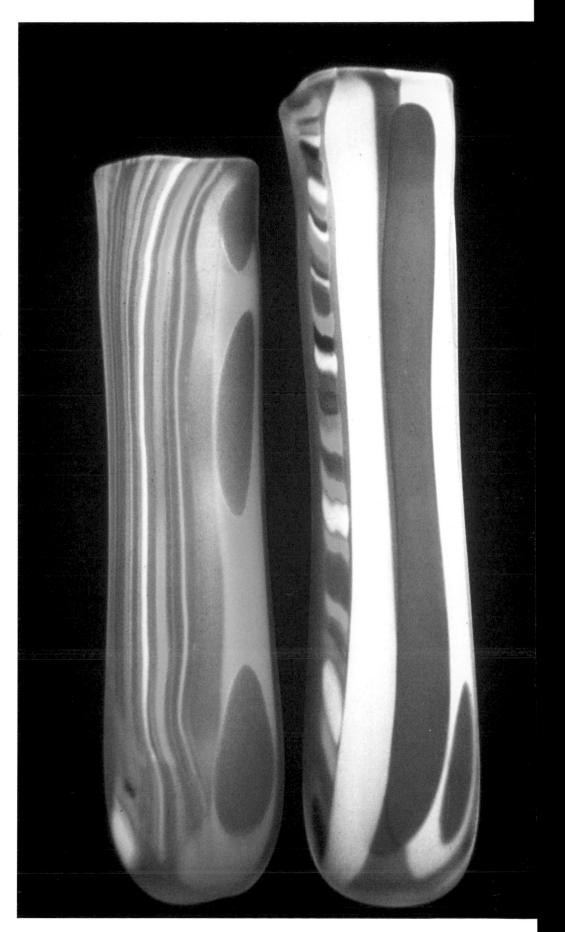

Vases
"Xela Collection."
Height up to 75cm (29.5in)
To commission only

02.07 | Everglassting Hot Glass Studio

Susan Nixon
Broadfield House
Glass Museum
Compton Drive
Kingswinford
West Midlands DY6 9NS
England
Tel: +44 1384 271048
Fax: +44 1384 812746

Education
BA (Hons)
3D Design (Glass),
University of Wolverhampton,
England, 1997

Collections/commissions
Six awards made for the
Eurovision Song Contest,
1998
Broadfield House Glass
Museum, Kingswinford,
West Midlands,
England, 1998

Vase
"Golden Eye." Blown glass with polished lenses
and sand-blasted and brush-polished finish.
35 x 10cm (14 x 4in)
In production

Decorative vessel
"Blue Veil Bowl." Blown glass with silver leaf, capturing
lettering within a depth of glass using stencilling techniques.
Personal choice of words available on commission.
14 x 10cm (5.5 x 4in)
To commission only

"THE WORK ENCAPSULATES A THOUGHT
THROUGH THE WRITTEN WORD
WITHIN A SCULPTURAL GLASS BOWL,
INVITING THE VIEWER TO INVESTIGATE
THE HIDDEN CONCEPTS WITHIN EACH PIECE."

Vases

Hand-blown lead-crystal vases, hand-finished to give a fine satin effect. Tall and elegant in form, with double curves on two of three sides and heavy base for stability.
34 x 10cm (13.25 x 4in)
In production

02.08	Katy Holford

8 Luton Road
Toddington
Bedfordshire LU5 6DF
England
Tel: +44 1525 872308
Fax: +44 1525 872308

Education
BA (Hons) Multi-Disciplinary Design,
North Staffordshire Polytechnic,
Stoke-on-Trent,
England, 1988
MA (RCA) Glass & Ceramics,
Royal College of Art,
London, England, 1992

Collections/commissions
Silver helical mirrors,
Claridges Hotel,
London, England, 1997
Copper-leaf large serpentine mirror, Yeeling Cheng,
London, England, 1997
The Cut Flowers range,
design and development
for manufacture by
Stuart Crystal,
England, 1996–98

02.09	First Glass	**Bob Crooks**

Unit 2a
Union Court
18-22 Union Road
Clapham
London SW4 6JP
England
Tel: +44 171 622 3322
Fax: +44 171 622 2563

Education
BA (Hons) Glass Design,
West Surrey College of Art &
Design, Farnham,
England, 1989

Collections/commissions
Crafts Council,
permanent collection,
London, England, 1995
Victoria & Albert Museum,
permanent collection,
London, England, 1996
Commission to design and
make the ABSA awards,
London, England, 1997

Bowl
"Encalmo Spirale." Clear and cased glass, hand-made in two
parts and joined halfway through the hot process with trailed
coloured spiral and complementary applied rim.
Dia. 39cm (15.5in)
To commission only

02.10 **Emily Jackson**

317 Hordern Road
Whitmore Reans
Wolverhampton
West Midlands WV6 0HE
England
Tel: +44 1902 564203 or
+44 1902 532881

Education
BA (Hons) 3D Design
(Glass),
University of Wolverhampton,
England, 1997

Bowl
"Nest." Pulled glass canes
cut, constructed and kiln-
fused using sand-box
technique. Finished with
real twigs.
25 x dia. 30cm
(10 x 12in)
In production

Bowl
Kiln-formed laminated glass
bowl with inclusions of silver
and schlag gold leaf with
fused glass grains.
5 x dia. 60cm (2 x 23.5in)
To commission only

02.11 **Sara F. A. McDonald**

4 Chestnut Street
Lincoln LN1 3HB
England
Tel: +44 1522 567124

Education
BA (Hons) 3D Design (Glass),
Surrey Institute
of Art & Design,
Farnham, England, 1987
MA Art & Design (Glass),
University of Wolverhampton,
England, 1996

Collections/commissions
Victoria & Albert Museum,
permanent collection,
London, England, 1989
Crafts Council,
permanent collection,
London, England, 1990
Museum of Applied Arts,
permanent collection,
Tallinn, Estonia, 1993

Vessel
"Deep Blue Sphere."
Made of recycled glass
using *pâte-de-verre*
technique combined with
ingredients from ceramics
industry to produce
distinctive textured glass.
24 x dia. 40cm
(9.5 x 15.75in)
In production

02.12 **Emma O'Dare** Balls Pond Studio
8b Culford Mews
London N1 4DX
England
Tel: +44 171 923 4736
Fax: +44 171 275 0401

Education
BA (Hons) 3D Design
(Glass with Ceramics),
University of Sunderland,
England, 1994

Collections/commissions
Montreal Museum of
Decorative Arts,
permanent collection,
Montreal, Canada, 1997

| 02.13 | Tobias Glass | **Lharne Tobias Shaw** |

Lharne Tobias Shaw
Units 2, 3 & 4
NCDA Workshops
Dunkirk Road
Dunkirk
Nottingham NG7 2PH
England
Tel: +44 1159 223314
Fax: +44 1159 705877

Education
BA (Hons) Fine Art,
Stourbridge College of Art &
Technology, England, 1987

Collections/commissions
Kiln-cast glass spiral blue
bowl, Castle Museum,
Nottingham, England, 1993
Kiln-cast glass spiral clear
bowl, Museum für Kunst und
Gewerbe, Hamburg,
Germany, 1995
Large six-pleat dish for
Sir Terence Conran,
London, England, 1995

Large six-pleat dish and small six-pleat dish
Both dishes in soda-lime float glass, draped by kiln-forming,
then sand-blasted on the reverse.
Small 8 x 29 x 32cm (3.25 x 11.5 x 12.5in)
Large 10 x 38 x 48cm (4 x 15.25 x 18.75in)
In production

"AN INTEREST IN
MODERN DESIGN
IS BEGINNING TO DEFINE
A NEW BUYING PUBLIC,
ENSURING THAT THE
NEXT MILLENNIUM
CAN BEGIN WITHOUT
THE SPECTRE OF
POSTWAR
INDIFFERENCE."

Vase
Single-handed vase.
Glass, cast and blown.
22 x 32 x 25cm
(8.5 x 12.5 x 9.75in)
To commission only

02.14 **Bruno Romanelli** 24 Stockwell Gardens
London SW9 0RX
England
Tel: +44 171 274 2871
Fax: +44 171 274 2871

Education
BA (Hons) Glass Design,
Staffordshire Polytechnic,
England, 1991
MA (RCA) Ceramics & Glass,
Royal College of Art,
London, England, 1995

Collections/commissions
Ernsting Foundation,
Alter Hof Herding,
Germany, 1995–97

02.15 | tranSglass

Tord Boontje and Emma Woffenden
179b Peckham Rye
London SE15 3HZ
England
Tel: +44 171 277 8394
Fax: +44 171 277 8394

Education
Tord Boontje — MA (RCA)
Industrial Design,
Royal College of Art,
London, England, 1994
Emma Woffenden — MA
(RCA) Glass & Ceramics,
Royal College of Art,
London, England, 1993

Jug and glasses
Used wine and beer
bottles. Cut with a diamond
saw, ground, polished, sand-
blasted.
Jug 27 x 7cm
(10.5 x 2.75in)
Glasses 8.2 x 5.8cm
(3.25 x 2.25in)
In production

Vase
Hand-made lead crystal.
Decoration eroded into
colour layers by sand-
blasting.
*32 x dia. 28cm
(13 x 11in)
To commission only*

02.16	Ruth Dresman

The Meads
West Knoyle
Warminster
Wiltshire BA12 6AE
England
Tel: +44 1747 830085

Education
BA (Hons) 3D Design,
Surrey Institute of Art &
Design, Farnham,
England, 1984

Collections/commissions
Installation of wall sculpture
at Salisbury District Hospital,
England, 1995
Contemporary ceramics and
glass collection,
Castle Museum Nottingham,
England, 1996
Private architectural
commission, Frome,
Somerset, England, 1997

Vessel
"Typographic series no. 2."
Cast in full lead crystal via
lost-wax process, with acid
and mechanical polished
finish.
25 x dia. 11cm
(10 x 4.25in)
Limited edition of 50

02.17 **Richard Vankoningsveld**

52 Tynemouth Road
Mitcham
Surrey CR4 2BN
England
Tel: +44 181 648 5113
E-mail:
glasform@dircon.co.uk
Website:
www.users.dircon.co.
uk/~glasform

Education
BA (Hons) Ceramics & Glass,
Buckinghamshire College,
High Wycombe, England,
1997

Collections/commissions
Blackheath Gallery,
London, England, 1997
Plateaux Gallery,
Tower Bridge Piazza,
London, England, 1997
Open Eye Gallery,
Edinburgh, Scotland, 1997

02.18 **Julian Stocks**

46 Kepler Road
London SW4 7PQ
England
Tel: +44 171 738 6279

Education
BA (Hons)
Public Art & Design,
Chelsea College of Art,
London, England, 1991
MA Public Art & Design,
Chelsea College of Art,
London, England, 1997

Collections/commissions
"Man and Nature," steel and
stained-glass screen,
Croxley Centre, Watford,
England, 1990
"The Grizedale Window,"
Theatre in the Forest,
Grizedale, Cumbria,
England, 1993
Etched and side-lit diptych,
St Bride's Church,
Fleet Street, London,
England, 1996

Glass sculpture
"Equilibrium." Glass
sculpture, cantilevered out
from foyer wall of SmithKline
Beecham Headquarters,
Harlow, Essex, England.
Illuminated by side lighting
and constructed entirely
from glass using latest glass-
bonding technology.
200 x 200cm
(78.75 x 78.75in)
To commission only

03**Lighting**

Introduction
Michael Marriott

It may appear surprising that there is a much smaller number of entries in this section than in the Furniture chapter (see pages 208–261). This is perhaps accounted for by the more stringent European Union safety-testing requirements that have recently come into being for lighting products.

However, apart from this difference in quantity, the Furniture and Lighting chapters are similar in many ways, most notably in that the products shown are frequently generated by the same DIY manufacturing culture (see my comments in the introduction to the Furniture chapter on page 211).

Both chapters illustrate well the middle ground of batch-produced designs that lies somewhere between true mass-production and one-off making — a middle ground where the designers' understanding of materials and processes is combined with a kind of "craftyness".

The "crafty" elements can sometimes be quite literal, in the traditional sense of the word "craft". On other occasions they relate to modes and scales of production — in other words, the designers' intelligent approach to the appropriation and use of technologies and processes. More importantly, they reflect the quality of thinking and of ideas and their translation into production.

The inherent flexibility and responsiveness of this milieu means that ideas that are often difficult for large and bureaucratic organizations to swallow come to the world in a purer, faster and fresher form. This approach allows the designer to play with light a little more freely. Some of the freshest of the ideas generated are illustrated here.

Light
"Postcard" light. Designed
by Michael Marriott. Steel
tube post-card light, and
wire frame, beech base.
50 x 50 x 20cm (20 x 8 x 8in)
In production

Units no. 4 & 6
Ellsworth Street
Bethnal Green
London E2 0AX
England

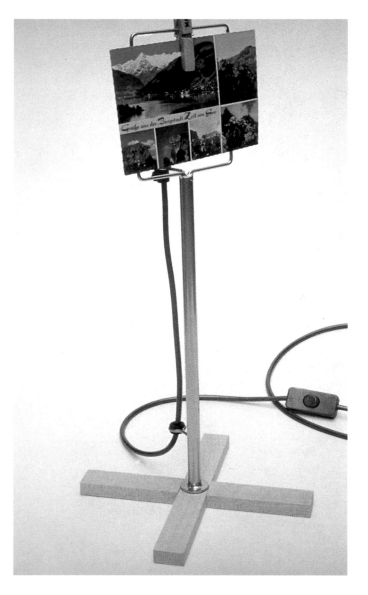

"THE MIDDLE GROUND OF
BATCH-PRODUCED DESIGNS
. . . LIES SOMEWHERE BETWEEN
TRUE MASS-PRODUCTION
AND ONE-OFF MAKING."

| 03.01 | Arkitype Design Partnership | **Douglas Bryden, Richard Smith and Stephen Young** |

1 Somerset Place
Charing Cross
Glasgow G3 7JT
Scotland
Tel:+44 141 333 1132
Fax:+44 141 333 1132

Education
Douglas Bryden,
Richard Smith and
Stephen Young —
all BA (Hons)
Product Design,
Glasgow School of Art,
Scotland, 1996

Collections/commissions
National Trust of Scotland
for The Hill House,
Helensburgh,
Scotland, 1998

"PEOPLE WALK PAST MY LAMP AND THINK IT'S JUST A LAMP IN THE SHAPE OF A STAR. I HAVE TO DRAG PEOPLE OVER AND SHOW THEM THE MAGIC."

| 03.02 | Pascal Anson |

48 Rennie Court
Upper Ground
London SE1 9LP
England
Tel:+44 171 620 0261
Fax:+44 171 620 0261

Education
BA (Hons) Furniture and
Product Design,
Kingston University,
England, 1995

Table light
"Solo table light." Cold-stamped polypropylene plastic. Flat-pack for self-assembly.
35 x 16.5 x 16.5cm
(13.75 x 6.5 x 6.5in)
In production

Lamp
"Stars in your Eyes."
Vacuum-formed plastic,
fluorescent tube,
CNC-routed mirror.
Dimension from point to
point 40 x 5cm depth
(15.75 x 2in)
In production

03.03	Azumi's

Shin and Tomoko Azumi
Ground Floor,
953 Finchley Road
London NW11 7PE
England
Tel: +44 181 731 7496
Fax: +44 181 731 7496

Education

Shin Azumi — BA (Hons)
Product Design, Kyoto City
University of Art,
Japan, 1989
MA (RCA) Industrial Design,
Royal College of Art,
London, England, 1994
Tomoko Azumi — BA (Hons)
Environmental Design,
Kyoto City University of Art,
Japan, 1989
MA (RCA) Furniture Design,
Royal College of Art,
London, England, 1995

Collections/commissions

Crafts Council, permanent
collection, London,
England, 1995
Geffrye Design Museum
collection, London,
England, 1996
Victoria & Albert Museum,
permanent collection,
London, England, 1997

Floor lamp

"Dimming with Movement" by Shin Azumi. Purpose of project
to associate — or rather combine — manipulation of object
with performance yielded. When handled, much like spinning
top, revolving around axis and dimming gradually. Design
both proposing new shape, and questioning old gesture of
turning on light. Beech, fire-proof paper, dimmer mechanism
and 40W bulb.
40 x dia. 22cm (15.75 x 8.5in)
To commission only

Lionel T. Dean
52 Rauceby Drove
South Rauceby
Lincolnshire NG34 8QB
England
Tel: +44 1529 488436
Fax: +44 1529 488437

Education
BSc (Hons) Mechanical
Engineering,
University of Hertfordshire,
England, 1985
MDes (RCA) Automotive
Design, Royal College of Art,
London, England, 1987

Recessed wall lamp
"Lampadina." Cast-aluminium reflector panel over simple wall
box, providing direct wall/ceiling or wall/floor wash as well as
indirect light from bulb-shaped reflector. Fitted with low-
voltage dichroic 10-35W bulbs and integral electronic
transformer. Received two international design awards —
Interieur '96, Belgium, and Expocasa, Turin, Italy, 1998.
20 x 13 x 2.5cm (8 x 5 x 1in)
Prototype

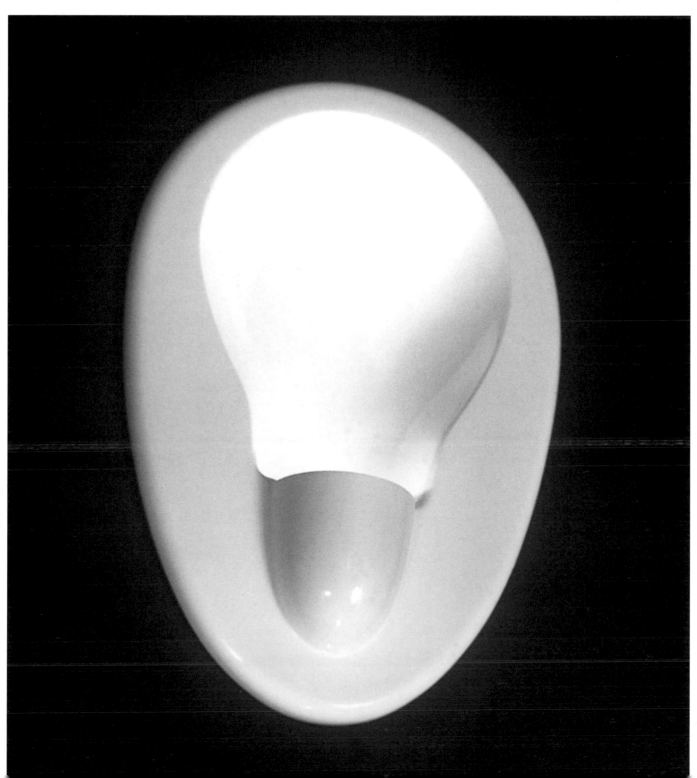

03.05   **Babylon Design Limited**   **Peter Wylly**
Unit 7, New Inn Square
1 New Inn Street
London EC2A 3PY
England
Tel: +44 171 729 3321
Fax: +44 171 729 3323

Education
BA (Hons) Fashion Design,
Middlesex University,
England, 1989

Collections/commissions
Conservatory tent,
Robert Bolt and Sarah Miles,
near Petersfield, England,
1990

"MODERNITY IS
THE WAY FORWARD;
THIS TIME WE NEED TO
BUILD FEELING
INTO THE FORM."

Floor lamp
"Eclipse 3." Biodegradable
polystyrene sheets cut and
formed into three layers of
lampshade, mild-steel
support and concrete base.
Height 196cm (77in)
Shade 64 x 38cm (25 x 15in)
In production

Floor and pendant lamps
"A Lighter Shade Up" and "A Lighter Shade Down," light and
shade series. Steel, satin chrome, limestone, dichroic halogen
reflector.
160 x 30 x 30cm (63 x 12 x 12in)
and 30 x 30 x 20cm (12 x 12 x 7.75in)
To commission only

03.06 | **Ralph Ball** | 177 Waller Road
London SE14 5LX
England
Tel: +44 171 635 8792
or +44 171 590 4323
Fax: +44 171 635 8792
or +44 171 590 4320

Education
MA (RCA) Furniture Design,
Royal College of Art,
London, England, 1980

Collections/commissions
Crafts Council,
permanent collection,
London, England, 1984
Museum of Modern Art,
permanent collection,
New York, USA, 1987

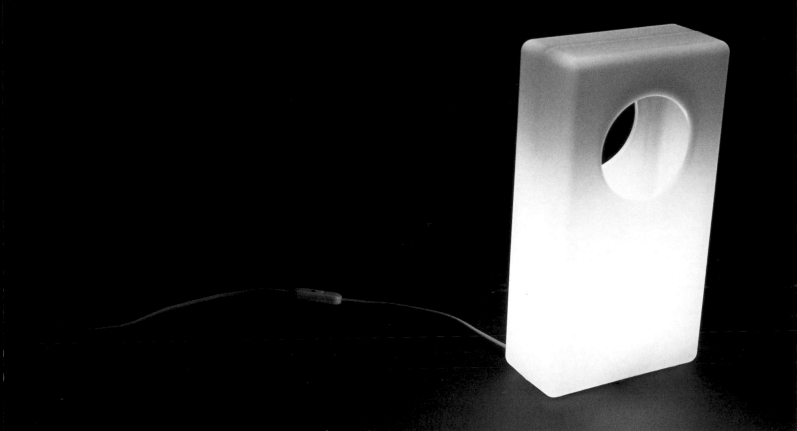

Table lamp
"Lio." Blow-moulded
polypropylene table lamp
challenging traditional lamp
format, with production
technology, material and
design contributing to
character, reminiscent of oil
cans and toy bricks.
Manufactured by
Driade, Italy.
37 x 19.5 x 11cm
(14.5 x 7.75 x 7.25in)
In production

Lampshade
Etched from a single sheet of
stainless steel. Simple
solution to everyday lighting
problem. Easy to install as an
up-lighter or down-lighter,
shielding light without hiding
the functional beauty of bulb
and fitting. Manufactured by
Radius, Germany.
12.5 x 36cm (5 x 14.25in)
In production

03.07 | **Bergne: design for manufacture**

Sebastian Bergne
2 Ingate Place
London SW8 3NS
England
Tel: +44 171 622 3333
Fax: +44 171 622 3336

Education
BA (Hons) Industrial Design
(Engineering),
Central St Martins College
of Art & Design,
London, England, 1988
MDes (RCA) Industrial
Design, Royal College of Art,
London, England, 1990

Collections/commissions
Lampshade,
Design Museum,
permanent collection,
London, England, 1996
Lampshade and "Spira"
flexible ballpoint pen, mutant
materials collection,
Museum of Modern Art,
New York, USA, 1996

Bodo Sperlein
145 de Beauvoir Road
London N1 4DL
England
Tel: +44 171 241 5204
Fax: +44 171 241 5202
E-mail: Lucysicks@aol.com

Education
BA (Hons) Ceramic Design,
Camberwell College of Art,
London, England, 1997

Collections/commissions
Plaster/bone china light
sculpture, Space,
London, England, 1997
Wall light installation,
Mission,
London, England, 1998

"I LIKE TO PROVE THE
VERSATILITY OF CERAMICS
AS A MATERIAL WHICH CAN BE APPLIED
IN UNUSUAL AREAS SUCH AS
FURNITURE AND LIGHTING,
TO PROVE CERAMICS CAN BE
GOOD MODERN DESIGN
BEYOND THE POTTER'S WHEEL."

Lights
"Light Sculpture." Sculptural
lights employing unique VPP
material —bone china mixed
with resin — enabling
material to be worked into a
large, thin, flat sheet,
textured by hand.
80 x 35cm (31.5 x 13.5in)
In production

Light shades
"Taco" pendant light shades, made from folded polypropylene sheet, produced in a variety of different colours and accepting bulbs of up to 100W.
Manufactured by Corkery Mackay Limited, England
45 x 15 x 30cm (17.75 x 6 x 11.75in), weight 360g (12.6oz)
In production

Inflatable light objects
"Luminosa" series 2.
Natural PVC inflatable envelope and compact fluorescent.
Height 102-202cm (47-86.5in), dia. 32-56cm (12.5-22in)
To commission only

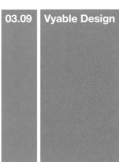

03.09	Vyable Design

Vyvyan Rose
The Moat Farm
Framlingham
Suffolk IP13 9JB
England
Tel: +44 7970 600186
Fax: +44 1728 621660

Education
BA (Hons) 3D Design,
Manchester Metropolitan
University, England, 1995

03.10	Katrien van Liefferinge

13 Armstrong Street
Leeds
West Yorkshire LS28 5BZ
England
Tel: +44 113 257 0241

Education
BA (Hons) 3D Design,
Leeds Polytechnic,
England, 1990
MA Art & Design,
Leeds Metropolitan University,
England, 1995

Collections/commissions
Royal Institute of British
Architects, London,
England, 1995
Kylie Minogue,
London, England, 1996
"Lux," North-West Arts
Board, Manchester,
England, 1998

Table lamps
Sheet polypropylene
with nickel-plated fixings.
27.5 x 18 x 16.5 cm
(11 x 7 x 6.5in)
In production

03.11	Bintang

Caroline Bromilow
1 Cockpit Yard
Cockpit Workshops
Northington Street
London WC1N 2NP
England
Tel: +44 171 916 2481
Fax: +44 171 916 2455

Education
BDes (Hons) Wood, Metal,
Plastics & Ceramics,
Liverpool Institute of Higher
Education, England, 1995

Collections/commissions
Collection for design
education, Geffrye Museum,
London, England, 1997
30 lamps for window display,
Garrards Crown Jewellers,
London, England, 1998

**Sharon Bowles and
Edgard Linares**
32 Hereford Road
London W2 5AJ
England
Tel: +44 171 229 9886
Fax: +44 171 229 9886

Education
Sharon Bowles — BA (Hons)
Interior Design,
Kingston Polytechnic,
England, 1982
Edgard Linares —
Diploma Fine Art, Taller 5,
School of Art,
Bogota, Colombia, 1983

"OUR DESIGNS STEM FROM
ARCHITECTURAL INFLUENCE
AND LIFELONG HISTORY OF
MANUFACTURING KNOWLEDGE.
WE WILL NOT BE
INFLUENCED BY TRENDS."

Floor lamps
"Espiga" floor lamp.
Available in three models:
EL/1 aluminium rods with
light source at base.
Height 200cm (78.75in)
EL/2 coppered steel rods
with light source at top.
Height 180cm (71in)
EL/3 coppered steel rods
with light source at base.
Height 90cm (35.5in)
In production

03.13	Regitze Bondesen

92 Sandbrook Road
London N16 0SP
England
Tel: +44 171 249 6580
Fax: +44 171 249 6580

Education
BA (Hons) Furniture Design
and Technology, London
Guildhall University,
England, 1993

Collections/commissions
Restaurant lighting, The
Lansdowne, Primrose Hill,
London, England, 1995
Dining room, 18-seater table
and matching mirror,
private client,
London, England, 1997
Dining table, half indoors and
half outdoors, private client,
Copenhagen, Denmark, 1998

Floor light
"Cylinderlight." Perforated
steel, acrylic discs and
dome, glass lamp.
*125 x dia. 75cm
(49.25 x 29.5in)
Limited edition*

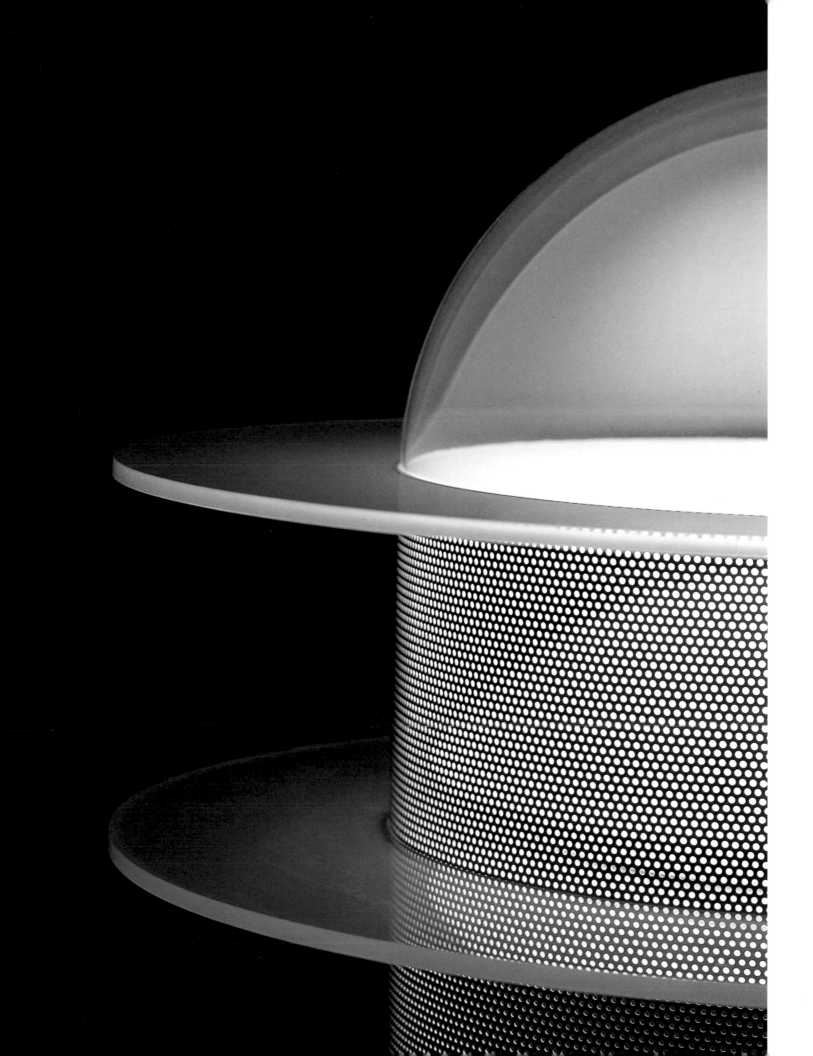

03.14 | **Cristina Lamíquiz Design**

Cristina Lamíquiz
53 Redcliffe Gardens
London SW10 9JJ
England
Tel: +44 171 373 5574
Fax: +44 171 373 5574
E-mail:
cld@c88c.demon.co.uk

Education
BA (Hons) Furniture &
Product Design,
Kingston University,
England, 1991
MA (RCA) Furniture Design,
Royal College of Art,
London, England, 1993

Collections/commissions
"Noodle" stools,
Blackburn collection,
London, England, 1993

"WILFUL PLAYFULNESS LOOKING AHEAD FOR THE ESSENCE OF FUNCTIONAL DESIGN."

Table lamp
"Emma" table light. PVC,
aluminium, 60W opal globe
lamp. Received special
judges' award, Muji, Tokyo,
Japan, 1995
*30 x 22 x 35cm
(12 x 8.5 x 13.75in)
In production*

Table lights
"Frodo, Gandalf, Sam Gamgee."
Hand-blown glass and metal springs.
50 x 30cm (19.75 x 12in)
In production

03.15	Rebecca Donaldson

Unit 6
Botley Flour Mill
Botley
Southampton
Hampshire SO30 2GB
England
Tel: +44 1489 796711

Education
BA (Hons) 3D Design (Glass),
Staffordshire University,
England, 1996

"I USE COLOUR, FORM AND MOVEMENT TO ENCOURAGE INTERACTION BETWEEN THE ONLOOKER AND THE PIECE."

Adjustable pendant lights
"Don't Run We Are Your Friends." Acrylic plastic.
19 x dia. 25cm (7.5 x 9.75in)
In production

| 03.16 | El Ultimo Grito | **Roberto Feo** |

Roberto Feo
26 Northfield House
Frensham Street
London SE15 6TL
England
Tel: +44 171 732 6614
Fax: +44 171 732 6614

Education
MA (RCA) Furniture,
Royal College of Art,
London, England, 1997

Collections/commissions
Review Gallery,
Design Museum,
London, England, 1997

03.17 | Inflate | **Nick Crosbie, Mark Sodeau and Nitzan Yaniv**
3rd Floor, 5 Old Street
London EC1V 9HL
England
Tel: +44 171 251 5453
Fax: +44 171 250 0311

Education
Nick Crosbie — MA (RCA)
Industrial Design,
Royal College of Art,
London, England, 1995
Mark Sodeau — BEng
(Hons) Aeronautical
Engineering, City University,
London, England, 1993
Nitzan Yaniv —
LLB (Hons) Law,
University of Birmingham,
England, 1993

Pendant light
"UFO." Inflatable, HF-welded, dip-moulded, vacuum-formed.
12 x dia. 45cm (4.75 x 17.75in)
In production

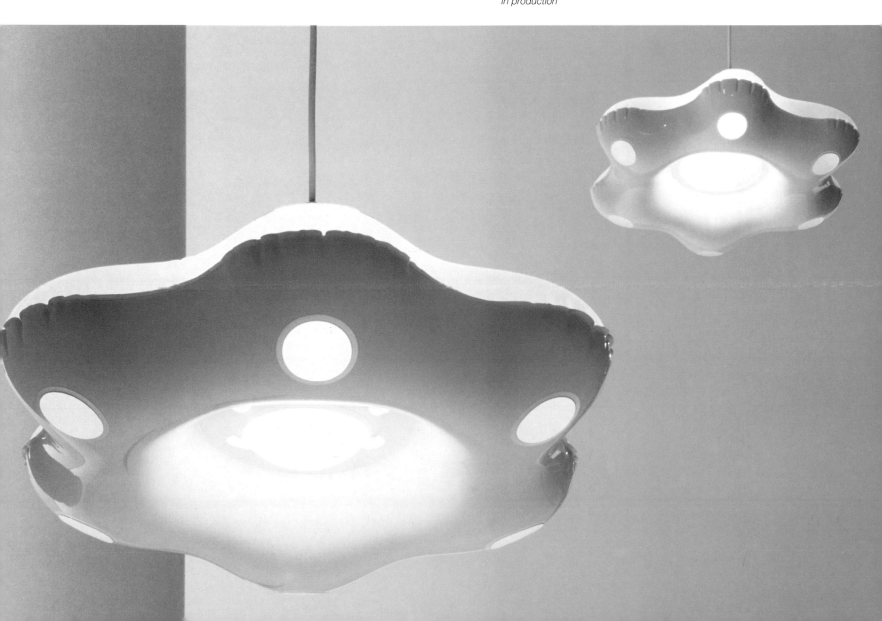

03.18　Greg James　The Signal Box
Bishopsgate Yard
Shoreditch High Street
London E1 6PD
England
Tel: +44 1223 812496
Fax: +44 171 613 2948

Education
BA (Hons) 3D Design &
Furniture,
Middlesex University,
England, 1991
MA (RCA) Furniture,
Royal College of Art,
London, England, 1995

Collections/commissions
Piers Gough,
"New Constellations,"
London, England, 1991
John Ryle, bureau,
London, England, 1997
Point-of-sale display units,
Ellipsis Publishing House,
throughout Britain, 1998

Floor light
"New Constellations — Concorde, Jumbo Jet." Aluminium,
nylon, silk-screened paper lampshade, plastic "Smartie" tops.
110 x dia. 54cm (43.25 x 21.25in)
To commission only

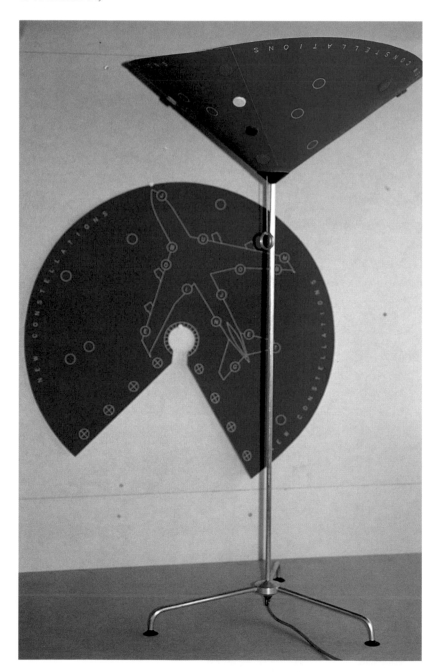

Floor light
"Lole." Stamped mirrored polyester film, folded around bulb supporting "bridge," giving 100 per cent reflection when off and infinite internal reflections when illuminated.
48 x 14.5 x 10cm (19 x 5.75 x 4in)
In production

| 03.19 | Andrew Woolnough | 104 Dalling Road
Hammersmith
London W6 0JA
England
Tel: +44 181 741 1338 |

Education
BA (Hons) 3D Design,
University of Plymouth,
Devon, England, 1997

| 03.20 | Tom Kirk | 13c Camberwell Church Street
London SE5 8TR
England
Tel: +44 171 780 9288
Fax: +44 171 780 9288

Education
BA (Hons) Silversmithing & Metalwork,
Camberwell College of Art,
London, England, 1994

Collections/commissions
Vijay's bar/restaurant,
Sheffield, England, 1997
Bar Jerusalem,
Rathbone Place,
London, England, 1998

Table light
"CS2." Cast-aluminium base, sandblasted diffuser.
60 x dia. 10cm
(23.5 x 4in)
In production

03.21	Lamp Art	**Adele Goulty and** **Michelle Cleary**

Oakwood
Petworth Road
Chiddingfold
Surrey GU8 4UJ
England
Tel: +44 1428 685472
Fax: +44 1428 684658

Education
Adele Goulty — BA (Hons)
3D Design, Surrey Institute
of Art & Design, Farnham,
England, 1995

Table lamp
Slip-cast ceramic base. Shape enabling lamps to be placed
on narrow surfaces.
77 x 40 x 16.5cm (30.25 x 15.75 x 6.5in)
In production

Chandelier
"Orbital." Available in white, yellow, orange, red, blue or green. Made from machine-stitched PVC, copper, brass and halogen bulbs.
150 x 150 x 100cm (59 x 59 x 39.5in)
To commission only

Lindsay Bloxam
Unit 1.03, Oxo Tower Wharf
Bargehouse Street
London SE1 9PH
England
Tel: +44 171 633 9494
Fax: +44 171 633 9494

Education
BA (Hons) Textiles/Fashion,
University of Central
England,
Birmingham, England, 1992
MA Textiles/Fashion,
University of Central
England,
Birmingham, England, 1995

Collections/commissions
Lighting sculpture,
Oxo Tower Wharf,
London, England, 1997
Lighting sculpture,
Stratford Picture House,
Stratford-upon-Avon,
England, 1997
Lighting sculpture, Liberty's,
London, England, 1998

Lampshade
"Chevron" pendant shade. Machine-stitched PVC flat-pack
shades. Available in white, yellow, red, blue or green.
Compatible with tungsten and energy-saving lightbulbs, and
with British and Continental fittings.
65 x 65 x 40cm (25.5 x 25.5 x 15.75in)
In production

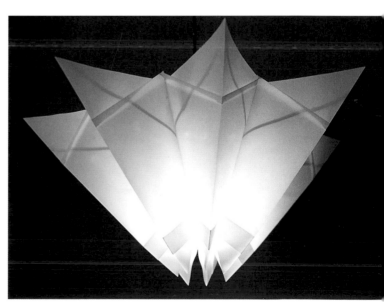

Table light
"Rubber Lamp." Heat-resistant rubber with beech stand.
40 x 10 x 20cm
(15.75 x 4 x 8in)
Prototype

03.23 Mark Bond Design

Mark Bond
Prism Design Studio
38 Grosvenor Gardens
London SW1W 0EB
England
Tel: +44 171 730 3011
Fax: +44 171 730 3011

Education
MA (RCA) Furniture Design,
Royal College of Art,
London, England, 1994

Collections/commissions
Tableware, Habitat Products,
London, England, 1994–98
The Design Museum shop,
café and Review Gallery,
London, England, 1997
Design of reception interior
and accompanying furniture
(tables, coffee tables),
CIA Media, London,
England, 1997-98

03.24 | **Neil Austin**

37 John Campbell Road
London N16 8JY
England
Tel: +44 171 241 2138
Fax: +44 171 241 2138
E-mail: neil@austin-england.demon.co.uk

Education
BA (Hons) Furniture Design,
Buckinghamshire Chiltern
University College,
England, 1980

Collections/commissions
"Valentine Vista," folding
table, Crafts Council,
London, England, 1996
"Youngman" stepladder
chair, Crafts Council,
London, England, 1996

Light
"Cup Light." Plastic cups, rivets, steel, electrical fittings.
Natural geometry.
Dia. 60cm (24in)
To commission only

03.25 Sharon Marston

Studio 54
1 Clink Street
Soho Wharf
London SE1 9DG
England
Tel: +44 171 234 0832
Fax: +44 171 357 6844

Education
BA (Hons) Jewellery,
Middlesex University,
England, 1992

Collections/commissions
Commissioned to design
pieces for window display,
Tiffany & Co., London,
England, 1997
National Trust for Scotland,
The Hill House,
Helensburgh,
Scotland, 1998

Floor lamp
Sculptural floor lamp in woven nylon and nylon monofilament,
stretched and sewn together.
150 x dia. 30cm (59 x 11.75in)
To commission only

Projection lamp

"Projection Lamp." Image of standard dichroic bulb projected onto ceiling by lens. Materials — lens, bulb, bicycle spokes, filter gel, lampshade wire.
Height 35cm (13in)
In production

| 03.26 | Ian McChesney | 20 Hayes Court Camberwell New Road London SE5 0TQ England Tel: +44 171 703 3461 |

Education
BA (Hons) 3D Design,
Kingston University,
England, 1994
MA (RCA) Architecture &
Interior Design,
Royal College of Art,
London, England, 1996

03.27 | **Neil Poulton** | 15 rue de l'Aqueduc
Paris 75010
France
Tel: +33 1 40 369 191
Fax: +33 1 40 369 292

Education
BSc Industrial Design
(Technology),
Napier University,
Edinburgh, Scotland, 1985
MA Design,
Domus Academy,
Milan, Italy, 1988

Collections/commissions
"Surf" suspension lighting
system for Artemide
Architectural/Megalit,
Italy, 1998
Collection of stacking
restaurant chairs ("Back Up,"
"Big Ears," "Blue Bud" and
"Bee"), for Allermuir Contract
Furniture Ltd., Darwen,
Lancashire, England, 1998

Wall light
"Surf." Die-cast aluminium piece available in white, black
or metallized grey. Light source either 300W (maximum)
halogen lamp or 18W compact fluorescent lamp.
30 x 17cm (12 x 6.75in)
In production

Pendant lights
Vacuum-formed. Hips, press studs, low-energy
compact fluorescent bulbs.
28 x dia. 42cm (11 x 16in)
In production

03.28 | **Sam Design Limited** | **Simon Maidment**
Basement
108 Huddleston Road
Islington
London N7 0EG
England
Tel: +44 171 272 8294
Fax: +44 171 272 8294

Education
MA (RCA) Furniture,
Royal College of Art,
London, England, 1992

Collections/commissions
"Baby Tambour" chair,
Vitra Design Museum,
permanent collection,
Weil am Rhein, Germany,
1998

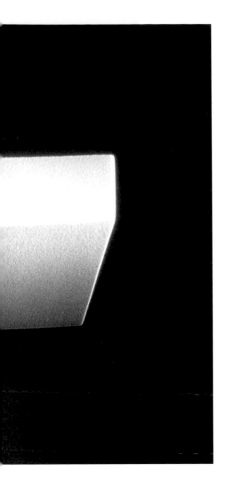

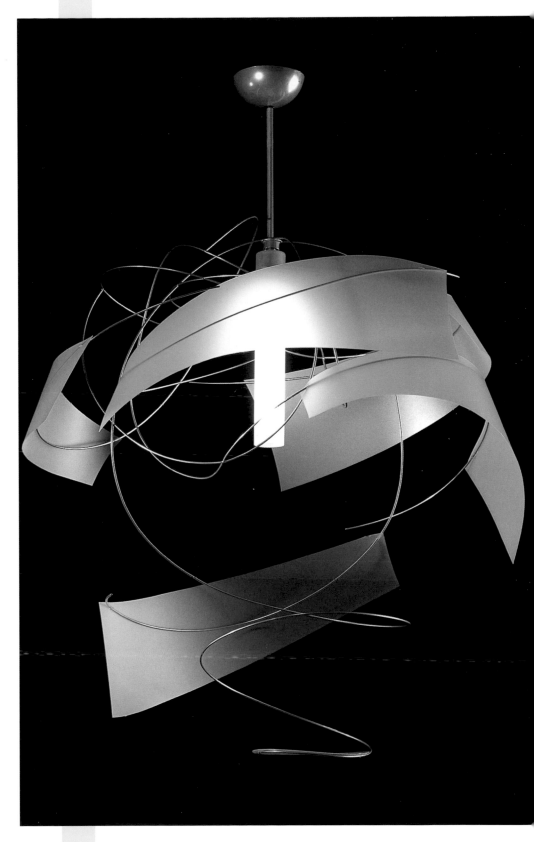

03.29	Suspect

Anthony Dickens
164 Palmers Road
London N11 1SN
England
Tel: +44 181 361 6715

Education
BA (Hons) Furniture &
Related Product Design,
Buckinghamshire College,
England, 1997

Collections/commissions
Jamies Bars for
the Design Solution,
London, England, 1998

Pendant light
"Senecio." Silver powder-coated wire frame with coloured
polypropylene "sails" attached with mini-elastic bands.
Compact fluorescent light source with sand-blasted glass cover.
80 x dia. 73cm (31.5 x 28.75in)
In production

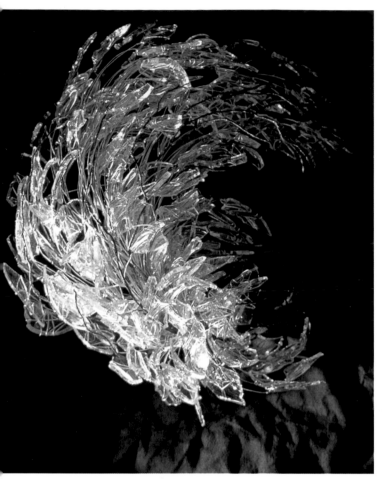

03.30 Deborah Thomas 323 Grove Green Road
Leytonstone
London E11 4EB
England
Tel: +44 181 519 2358

Education
BA (Hons) Fine Art,
Wolverhampton Polytechnic,
England, 1979
Postgraduate Higher
Diploma, Theatre Design,
Slade School of Fine Art,
London, England, 1983

Collections/commissions
Light for the Chairman's
conservatory,
Unilever House,
London, England, 1997
Three lights commissioned
for "The Cutting Edge"
exhibition,
Victoria & Albert Museum,
London, England, 1997
Suspended glass wall for
architect Charles Brown's
private collection,
Newbury, England, 1998

Chandelier/wall light
"Frozen Branch." Broken fragments of glass (green), steel wire,
steel rod, papier-mâché, inks, varnishes. Halogen lights.
50 x 50 x 15cm (19.5 x 19.5 x 6in)
To commission only

03.31 Totem Design London **Ian Hume and
Julian Turner**
2 Alexander Street
London W2 5NT
England
Tel: +44 171 243 0692
Fax: +44 171 243 0692

Education
Ian Hume — BA (Hons),
RIBA Part I,
Liverpool University,
England, 1992
BArch,
Manchester University,
England, 1992
Julian Turner — RIBA, Part II,
Architectural Association,
London, 1989

Collections/commissions
Bar Design, Vinyl Bar,
Camden, London, England,
1996
Redesign of bar including
lighting and chandelier,
Jimmie's Wine Bar,
Kensington,
London, England, 1997

Floor lights
"Zip-Code." Wire-framed
lights with various patterned
rip-stop nylon sailcloth
covers zipped onto frame.
Durable, colourful, and easily
changeable. Fully collapsible
for easy packaging and
export. Range including
Bondi, Brighton, Pacific and
Ipenema patterns. Three
sizes available.
Height 46-145cm (18-57in)
In production

Woven light
Nickel-plated trade frame
with woven stainless steel
wire, lathe-turned aluminium
base, in-line switch. Light
source: small E14 Edison
screw, 25W clear 4.5cm
round bulb.
Small version 23 x dia. 9 cm
(9 x 3.5in)
Large version 36 x dia. 10cm
(14 x 4in)
In production

03.32 | **MY-022**

Michael Young
c/o TYMC London
Unit 3a
101 Farm Lane
London SW6 1QJ
England
Tel: +44 171 610 0799
Fax: +44 171 386 9584
E-mail: tymc@dial.pipex.com

Education
BA (Hons) Furniture Design,
Kingston University,
England, 1992

Collections/commissions
Mid-90s Modern Furniture
Collection for E&Y Ltd,
Tokyo, Japan, 1995
Design Museum,
permanent collection,
London, England, 1996
Atelier des Enfants,
Centre Pompidou,
Paris, France, 1996

04 **Floor Coverings**

Introduction
Jane Priestman

Floors affect our lives at every level, from cradle to grave as a constant background to our lives and there has never been a time of greater opportunity for both client and designer to enrich our lives with quality surfaces, both externally and internally.

As the world appears smaller to a sophisticated travelling public, so the influences from abroad are absorbed and translated into materials offering wider possibilities for the use of pattern, texture, colour and design – consider the joy, for instance, of tiled floors from Spain and Mexico, mosaics from Italy and India, patterned stone pavements from Portugal, rich hand-woven rugs from Turkey and the Middle East, contemporary floor rugs from the USA and Australia, and now breakthroughs in computer design for carpets in public areas such as airports and railway terminals.

At the same time the demand for urban renewal of city centres has encouraged manufacturers to develop ranges of coloured concrete bricks and detailing. Landscape designers now have wide choices in practical, but decorative, blocks for pavements, forecourts, patios and hard-use public spaces. If used in conjunction with a professional designer, such as Tess Jaray (Wakefield and Victoria Stations) or Chris Tipping (see page 111) (Royal College of Art, London and promenade at Bridlington, Yorkshire), our lives are truly enriched.

Detail from a rug by
Lorraine Statham
(see page 107)

And in the most unexpected places, floors are taking prominence.
The spectacular, lit perspex catwalk installed by Alexander McQueen
for London Fashion Week hovered above tanks of water into which
black ink was sprayed at intervals.

At a more mundane level, quartz-resin floors not only respond to
hygiene and safety standards for durable, slip-resistant, easy-to-clean
seamless flooring, but now offer vibrant colours for factories, kitchens
areas, warehouses and sports halls. Linoleum can be cut and spliced
into exotic patterns and motifs, and so elevated to use in more formal
interiors.

In the domestic arena, the trend towards hard flooring, as opposed
to wall-to-wall carpet, has opened up a market for the individually
designed rug related to interior design schemes. These can range
from minimalist hand-weave, such as Jason Collingwood's rugs (see
page 102), to exuberant tufted extravaganzas such as those of
Annette Nix (see page 109), with every possibility in between.

Opportunities therefore abound for new young designers. I wish them
firm footings for the future.

"THERE HAS NEVER BEEN A TIME OF GREATER OPPORTUNITY FOR BOTH CLIENT AND DESIGNER TO ENRICH OUR LIVES WITH QUALITY SURFACES, BOTH, EXTERNALLY AND INTERNALLY."

04.01   **Lucy Wassell**   140b New North Road
London N1 7BH
England
Tel: +44 171 226 5560
Fax: +44 171 729 6768

Education
BA (Hons) Textiles (Fashion),
Manchester Polytechnic,
England, 1989

Collections/commissions
Collection of children's rugs,
Kappa Lambda Rugs,
London, England, 1997
Private commission,
Drusilla Beyfus and
Milton Schulman,
London, England, 1998
Private commission,
Felicity Green Hill,
London, England, 1998

Hand-tufted rug
"Jump." 100 per cent wool, hand-tufted rug. Designed and in
production for Kappa Lambda Rugs, London, England.
185 x 105cm (73 x 41.5in)
In production

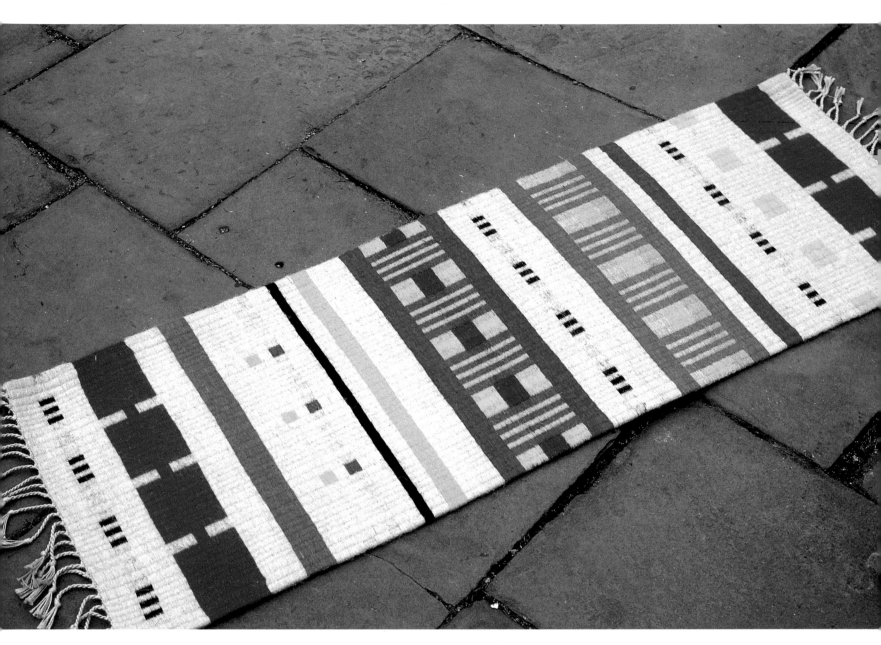

Hand-woven rug

Hand-woven with wool weft and strong linen warp, to create very durable fabric. Including Soumak and Damascus edge finish, with threads sewn back into body of rug. All rugs reversible.

60 x 120cm (24 x 48in)

To commission only

04.02	Laura Watts

35 Granton Avenue
Upminster
Essex RM14 2RU
England
Tel: +44 1708 441611

Education
BA (Hons) Woven Textiles,
Surrey Institute of Art &
Design, Farnham, England,
1997

Collection/commissions
Floor rug,
private commission,
Bournemouth, England,
1998
Floor rug,
private commission,
Middlesex, England, 1998

"MY RUG DESIGNS EXPRESS
SUBTLE VARIATIONS
IN WHICH COLOURS,
SHAPES AND LINES ARE POISED
IN DELICATELY BALANCED
RELATIONSHIPS."

Linoleum floor covering
"A Colourful Journey." Throughout ground floor of Doncaster
Community Arts, England. Produced by Furbo-Nairn.
350 x 350cm (137 x 137in)
In production

| 04.03 | Usha | Usha Mahenthiralingam |

Usha Mahenthiralingam
House of Hearts
15 Lord Nelson Street
Sneinton
Nottingham NG2 4FA
England
Tel: +44 1159 118353

Education
BA (Hons) Printed Textiles,
Loughborough College of Art
& Design, England, 1985

Collections/commissions
Four prints,
Rampton Prison,
England, 1993
Banners, "Gardens in the
sky," Belgrave Library,
Leicester, England, 1994
Design of crèche,
Doncaster Community Arts,
Expressive Arts Room,
Doncaster, England, 1998

Natalie Woolf
10 Wharfedale Street
Leeds LS7 2LF
England
Tel: +44 113 262 7704
Fax: +44 113 237 4691

Education
BA (Hons) Fine Art, Leeds
Metropolitan University,
England, 1987

Collections/commissions
Street surface design and
public art piece, Garston
Village Design Competition,
as team member,
Bauman Lyons Architects,
Liverpool, England, 1997-99
Carpet for South Downs
Health Authority,
reception area,
Newhaven Hospital, East
Sussex, England, 1997-98
New café flooring and design
team member,
Russell Cotes Art Gallery
and Museum,
Bournemouth,
England, 1997-98

Floor tile
"Pebble." Vinyl tiles hand- or batch-
printed.
Manufactured by The Amtico Floor
Company, London, England.
30.5 x 30.5cm (12 x 12in)
In production

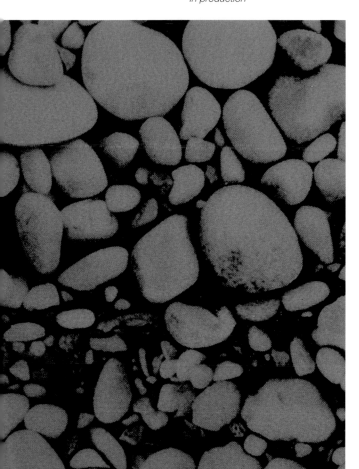

Floor covering
"Tropical Fruit Salad." Series
number 3. Hand-painted and
printed hard-surface floor
covering, sealed and
varnished with industrial
finishes, waxed for
maintenance.
60 x 160cm (24 x 63in)
To commission only

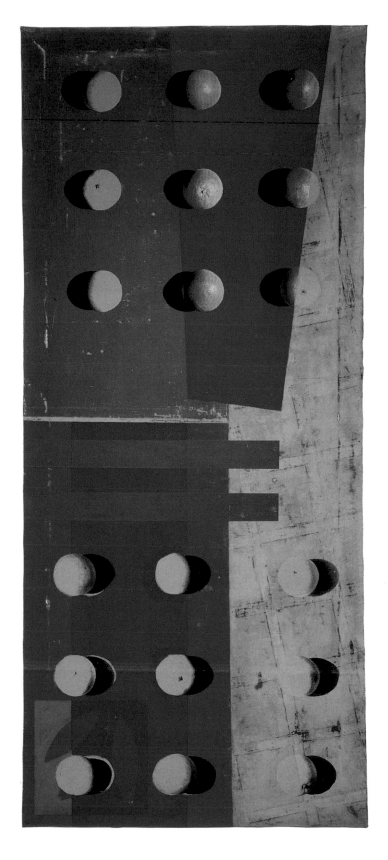

Hand-carved rug
"Krenkerup." Tufted wool,
hand-carved.
Dia. 180cm (71in)
To commission only

Hand-carved rug
"Crawley Down." Jute, tufted
and hand-carved.
210 x 165cm (84 x 65in)
To commission only

04.05 | Amazed | **Madeleine and
Dudley Edwards**
Tanfield House
Wighill Village
near York
North Yorkshire LS24 8BQ
England
Tel: +44 1937 832813
Fax: +44 1937 530730
E-mail:
madeleine@angeland.demon.
co.uk

Collections/commissions
Tori Amos, New York, USA,
1997
Jonathan Cainer, Daily Mail,
London, England, 1998
Botton Steiner School,
Camphill Village, Yorkshire,
England, 1998

182 Highbury Hill
London N5 1AU
England
Tel: +44 171 354 8676
Fax: +44 171 354 8676

Education
BA (Hons) Printed Textiles,
Edinburgh College of Art,
Scotland, 1983

Collections/commissions
Three painted, sand-washed
silk scarves, Crafts Council,
London, England, 1994
Painted fine wool shawl,
Contemporary Art Society,
London, England, 1995
Painted silk scarf,
Victoria & Albert Museum,
London, England, 1997

"THE POWER AND SEDUCTIVENESS
OF COLOUR IS A CONTINUING THEME,
CONCENTRATING ON RHYTHMS,
AREAS, PROPORTION AND TEXTURE.
THE AIM IS SIMPLICITY
AND QUIET STRENGTH."

Knotted rug
"Circle." Designed by Kate Blee, produced in Turkey through
Christopher Farr, London, England. Hand-dyed and
hand-knotted.
180 x 245cm (71 x 96.5in)
To commission only

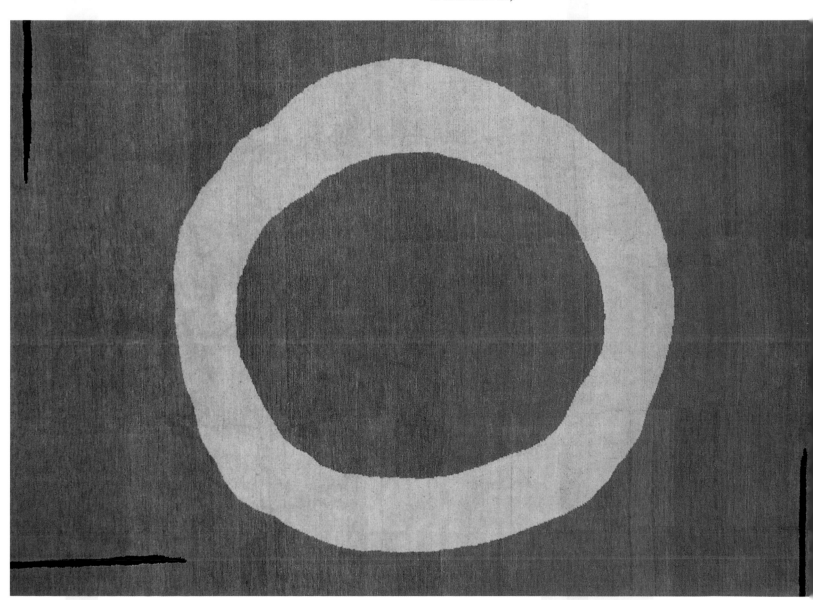

Shaft-switched rug
"No. 58." Wool, horsehair
and linen. Woven using
shaft-switching method.
200 x 100cm (78.75 x 39in)
To commission only

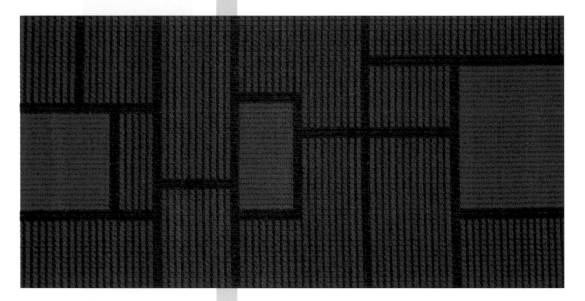

Shaft-switched rug
"No. 103." Wool, horsehair
and linen. Woven using
shaft-switching method.
200 x 100cm (78.75 x 39in)
To commission only

04.07 **Jason Collingwood** 31 Gladstone Road
Colchester
Essex CO1 2EA
England
Tel: +44 1206 502073
Fax: +44 1206 262401
E-mail:
jason@plysplit.demon.co.uk

Collections/commissions
Tate Gallery,
permanent collection,
London, England, 1991
Series of rugs for a castle in
Switzerland, commissioned
through an English interior
designer, 1991
24 rugs, Sheraton Hotel,
Dar-es-Salaam, Tanzania,
1995

04.10 | **Lisa Jones** | 110b Norwood Road
Herne Hill
London SE24 9BB
England
Tel: +44 181 678 7042
Fax: +44 181 678 7042

Education
BA (Hons) Constructed
Textile Design,
University of Central England,
Birmingham, England, 1992

Collections/commissions
Tufted rug,
Bolero Star yacht, 1993
Three rugs,
Royal Caribbean
International,
Oslo, Norway, 1997
Two runners for restaurant
interior, Camtos Architects,
for Pizza Express
Restaurant, London,
England, 1997

Gun-tufted rug
"Circle." Gun-tufted wool, hessian-backed, use of relief
surface for etched quality.
150 x 150cm (59 x 59in)
To commission only

04.11 Lynn Kirkwood Designs

Lynn Kirkwood
99 Giles Street
Leith
Edinburgh EH6 6BZ
Scotland
Tel: +44 131 555 2444
Fax: +44 131 555 2444

Education
BA (Hons) Printed Textiles,
Edinburgh College of Art,
Scotland, 1991
Diploma Design,
Edinburgh College of Art,
Scotland, 1992

Collections/commissions
Business Design Centre,
eight rugs commissioned,
London, England, 1996
Three rugs for the
Scottish Poetry Library,
Edinburgh, Scotland, 1998
Three rugs, Cairn Energy,
Edinburgh, Scotland, 1998

"INNOVATION IN FLOOR
DECORATION —
RUGS OF THE FUTURE ARE
NOT JUST FUNCTIONAL
FLOOR COVERINGS,
THEY ARE WORKS OF ART
IN THEIR OWN RIGHT."

Hand-tufted rug
Hand-gun-tufted rug, with
80 per cent wool and
20 per cent nylon.
157 x 146cm
(61.5 x 57.5in)
In production

Hand-made rug
"Vis-à-Vis." Part of "The
Manhattan Collection,"
hand-made from
100 per cent wool,
available in three sizes and
alternative colourways.
180 x 120cm (71 x 47in)
210 x 150cm (82.5 x 59in)
275 x 180cm (108 x 71in)
In production

"INNOVATIVE
DESIGN SHOULD
BE ACCESSIBLE
TO EVERYONE
WITH THE GOOD
TASTE TO
RECOGNIZE IT."

04.12 **Loop House**

Lorraine Statham
Park Royal Business Centre
9–17 Park Royal Road
London NW10 7LQ
England
Tel: +44 181 961 4950
Fax: +44 181 961 4950

Education
BA (Hons) Carpet & Floor
Covering Design,
Kidderminster College/
University of Wolverhampton,
England, 1992
Postgraduate Diploma,
Textiles, Manchester
Metropolitan University,
England, 1994

Collections/commissions
Rug, *Good Morning
Television*, BBC Pebble Mill,
England, 1995
Wall hangings for McDonalds
Restaurants Limited,
throughout the UK, 1992–96
Selfridges,
London, England, 1996
Slug & Lettuce plc,
bars and restaurants
throughout the UK, 1998

Hand-tufted rug
"Charlie." Hand-tufted wool.
180 x 122cm (71 x 48in)
To commission only

04.13 | **Michael Sodeau Partnership**

**Michael Sodeau and
Lisa Giuliani**
24 Rosebery Avenue
London EC1R 4SX
England
Tel: +44 171 837 2343
Fax: +44 171 837 2343

Education
Michael Sodeau — BA
(Hons) Product Design,
Central St Martins College
of Art & Design, London,
England, 1994

04.14 **Annette Nix** Top Flat
11 Estelle Road
London NW3 2JX
England
Tel: +44 171 377 2900
Fax: +44 171 482 0530

Education
BA (Hons) Textile Design,
Central St Martins College of
Art & Design,
London, England, 1986

Collections/commissions
London Electricity Board,
London, England, 1991
Warner Music International,
London, England, 1995
The Big Breakfast,
Channel Four Television,
London, England, 1995

Hand-tufted rug
"Something for the
Weekend." 100 per cent
wool hand-tufted rug with
inserts of wood, stone,
sandblasted glass, perspex
box mirror based with water.
*400 x 250cm
(157.5 x 98.5in)
To commission only*

Hand-tufted rug
"Squiggly." 100 per cent
wool hand-tufted rug with
polyrey inserts.
*500 x 90cm (197 x 35.5in)
To commission only*

Gun-tufted rug
"Borax." Gun-tufted rug commissioned by David Leon &
Partners for British Borax Ltd. One of a pair.
300 x 300cm (118 x 118in)
To commission only

Christopher Tipping

Clockwork Studios
38b Southwell Road
London SE5 9PG
England
Tel: +44 171 274 4116
Fax: +44 171 738 3743

Education
BA (Hons) Ceramics, Surrey
Institute of Art & Design,
Farnham, England, 1981
MA (RCA) Ceramics,
Royal College of Art,
London, England, 1985

Collections/commissions
Hard landscaping,
commissioned by East
Yorkshire Borough Council
and Humberside Arts,
consisting of patterned
coloured clay paviors, fish-
embossed and decorative
brick elevations, spanning
1,000 linear metres of
seafront promenade,
Bridlington, England,
1993–96
Painted murals to wall
elevations, Woodhouse
Tunnel, commissioned by
Leeds City Council and
Public Arts Wakefield, inner
ring road scheme,
Leeds, England, 1994
Integrated foyer and main
entrance,
Community Centre,
commissioned by Worcester
City Council Leisure Services
Department, Dines Green,
Worcester, England,
1997–98

Linoleum flooring
Hand-cut, inlaid linoleum floor covering, Millbrook Primary
School, Grove, Wantage, Oxfordshire. Commissioned by
Oxfordshire County Council Public Arts Officer, school
governors and W.S. Atkins Architects.
2 x 40m (6.5 x 130ft)
To commission only

04.16 **MY-022** **Michael Young**
c/o TYMC London
Unit 3a
101 Farm Lane
London SW6 1QJ
England
Tel: +44 171 610 0799
Fax: +44 171 386 9584
E-mail. tymc@dial.pipex.com

Education
BA (Hons) Furniture Design,
Kingston University, England,
1992

Collections/commissions
Mid-90s Modern Furniture
collection for E&Y Ltd,
Tokyo, Japan, 1995
Design Museum,
permanent collection,
London, England, 1996
Atelier des Enfants,
Centre Pompidou, Paris,
France, 1996

Woven rug
"MY014." 100 per cent woven wool. Two versions: dark blue,
pale blue and white or dark yellow, pale yellow and white.
140 x 140cm (55 x 55in)
In production

05Furnishing Textiles

Introduction
James Park

The textiles shown in the following pages demonstrate the enormous variety of attitudes and approaches by young designer-workers and textile artists in Britain at the end of the 20th century. The range of materials is equally large — from traditional natural yarns to the latest developments in fibres and finishes emerging from laboratories and industrial research initiatives. However, no matter how modern the minds and methods of the present day's textile-makers are, there is still a debt to be acknowledged to the aspirations of the Arts and Crafts Movement and the philosophy of the several Bauhaus establishments of the 1920s and 1930s in Germany. The connecting line has sometimes dwindled almost completely, but has survived thanks to the strength and example of the Bauhaus textile workshops and the women (and some men) who emerged from there, were dispersed throughout Europe and went on to teach and inspire generations of young people.

In Britain we must also acknowledge the inspiration and devotion to textiles of Ethel Mairet, Margaret Leischner and Marianne Straub. These three have influenced textile education nationally — Mairet from her workshop in Ditchling, Sussex, Leischner and Straub from the Royal College of Art and Middlesex University. Peter Collingwood must also be mentioned as a forerunner for his international reputation and

"I CONGRATULATE THE DESIGNERS WHOSE WORK IS SHOWN IN THIS CHAPTER. THEIR WORK IS PROFESSIONAL AND DESIRABLE."

achievement as a weave artist and his important technical books published over the last 30 years.

The restructuring of art education in the 1960s brought great benefits to the development of applied art and design. The new polytechnics were able to develop strongly focused departments and workshops, and to extend textile studies into fine art and mixed media, often combined with business studies. These persist and in most cases have shaped the education of the young designers represented here.

Financial pressures and the relocation of the textile industry in the UK have led to changes in conventional employment profiles. These have, in turn, forced emerging designers to create a "new" textile culture which helps young artists and craftsmen to survive and flourish. The help and encouragement of various funding bodies such as the Crafts Council, the Jerwood Prize for Applied Arts and the Worshipful Company of Weavers allow exhibitions and commissions to occur more frequently and readily than in the past. Small production units are also springing up, producing creative, desirable and viable textile works. And annual design events such as the Chelsea Crafts Fair and 100% Design give independent designers excellent opportunities to show and sell their work as well as to meet potential customers.

I congratulate the designers whose designs are shown in this chapter. Their work is professional and desirable. In many cases they have already established themselves as professional business companies who are now into the next stage of their development.

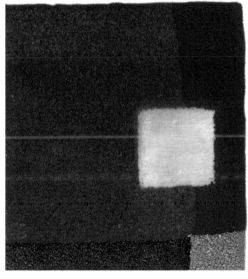

Detail from a wall hanging by
Tracy Hillier (see page 130)

05.01 | Suzanne Widdowson

6 Gaddesby Lane
Rearsby
Leicestershire LE7 4YJ
England
Tel: +44 1664 424875

Education
BA (Hons) Textiles,
Loughborough College of Art
& Design, England, 1997

Collections/commissions
Private collection,
New Britain,
Connecticut, USA, 1997
Public commission,
Community House,
Edmonton, London,
England, 1998
Private commission,
Kanne-Riemst,
Belgium, 1998

"PEOPLE ARE QUICK TO BUY PAINTINGS AT A GALLERY, THOUGH THEY PONDER WHEN THEY SEE OTHER NEW, FRESH, PURE DESIGN WHICH CAN REPLACE OIL OR WATERCOLOUR. THIS IS GRADUALLY CHANGING, THANKS TO THE GROWING NUMBER OF CONTEMPORARY DESIGN EXHIBITIONS AND LITERATURE."

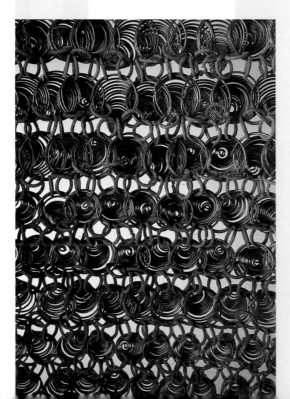

Interior hanging
Hand-formed copper spirals
of varying size connected
together with corroded
copper links.
60 x 180cm (23.5 x 70.75in)
To commission only

Wall hanging
Textile constructed with narrow strip-woven fabric using backed-cloth weave. Continuous strip cut to length and twisted before being recombined by sewing. Made from spun silk, wool and cotton, using acid and indigo dyes in the Ikat technique.
157 x 76cm (62 x 30in)
To commission only

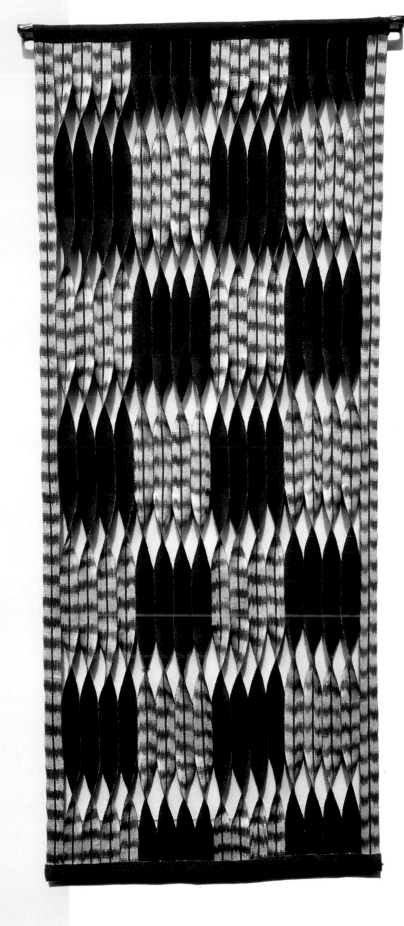

| 05.02 | Deirdre Wood |

28 Hyde Street
Winchester
Hampshire SO23 7DX
England
Tel: +44 1962 855463
Fax: +44 1962 855463

Education
BA (Hons) Woven Textiles, Surrey Institute of Art & Design, Farnham, England, 1995

Collections/commissions
Contemporary Art Society projects, three large wall hangings for BUPA House, London, England, 1996
Large wall hanging for Ena Bodin, Danish artist, London, England, 1997
Four ecclesiastical stoles for Rev. Terry Hemming, Winchester, England, 1997—98

Wall hanging/painting
"Red Skirt".
Dye on spun silk.
250 x 100cm (98.5 x 39.5in)
To commission only

05.03 **Carole Waller**

One Two Five
Bow Road
Bathford
Bath, Avon BA1 7LR
England
Tel: +44 1225 858888
Fax: +44 1225 858888

Education
BA (Hons) Painting,
Canterbury College of Art,
England, 1978
MA Fine Art Fibres,
Cranbrook Academy of Art,
England, 1982

Collections/commissions
Birmingham City Art Gallery,
England, 1995
Victoria & Albert Museum,
permanent collection,
London, England, 1997
Korean Biennale,
"Art to Wear",
permanent collection,
Kwangju City Museum,
Korea, 1998

05.04 | **Alison White** | 21 Kent Avenue
Ealing
London W13 8BE
England
Tel: +44 181 997 3238

Education
BA (Hons) Textile Design,
University of Derby,
England, 1998

Shower curtain
"Iris Petals Suspended in Ice". Heat transfer-printed onto textured man-made fabrics.
Repeat size 15 x 25cm (6 x 10in)
Prototype

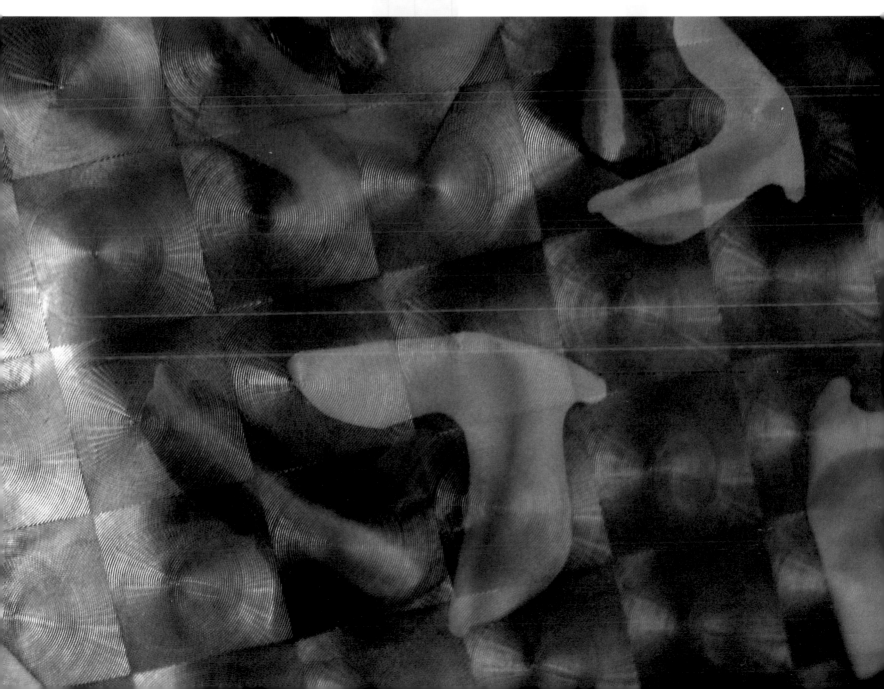

05.05 **Mavina Baker**

97 Park Road
Hampton Hill
Middlesex TW12 1HU
England
Tel: +44 181 979 5404
Fax: +44 181 941 9237

Education
BA (Hons) Textiles, Surrey
Institute of Art & Design,
Farnham, England, 1997

"THE CHALLENGE FOR HAND-WOVEN AND HAND-PRINTED TEXTILES IS TO BREAK THE GENERALLY HELD PERCEPTION OF TEXTILES AS CRAFT AND DRIVE TOWARDS A MORE COMMERCIAL IMAGE."

Curtain fabric
"Midsummer Curtain". Hand-
woven cloth made with very
fine bleached and
unbleached Irish linen.
Gauze technique used to
achieve light, translucent
fabric. Non-repeating pattern
for individual installation.
85 x 260cm (33.5 x 102.5in)
To commission only

Throws
"Fern" and "Mimosa".
Embroidered and felted
lambswool, hand-dyed.
150 x 150cm (59 x 59in)
*To commission and from
selected stockists*

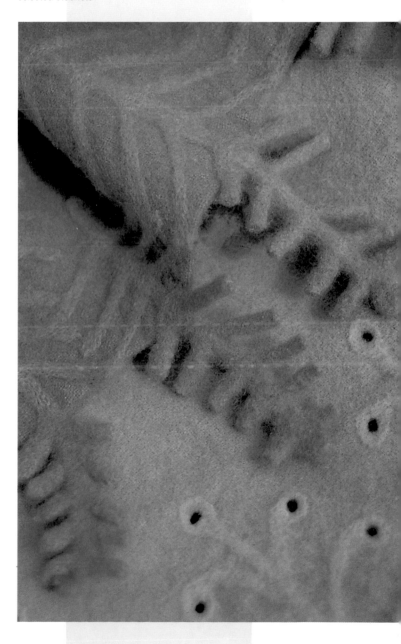

05.06 **Asta Barrington**

Studio A104
Riverside Business Centre
Haldane Place
London SW18 4LZ
England
Tel: +44 181 874 3001
Fax: +44 181 874 3001
E-mail: asta.barrington
@dial.pipex.com

Education
MA (RCA) Embroidery,
Royal College of Art,
London, England, 1995

Collections/commissions
Drawing room window
fabrics, "Living at Belsay",
Belsay Hall, Northumbria,
England, 1996

Wall hanging
Hand-rolled wool felt.
51 x 76cm (20 x 30in)
To commission only

05.07	Kate Blee

182 Highbury Hill
London N5 1AU
England
Tel: +44 171 354 8676
Fax: +44 171 354 8676

Education
BA (Hons) Printed Textiles,
Edinburgh College of Art,
Scotland, 1983

Collections/commissions
Three painted, sand-washed
silk scarves, Crafts Council,
London, England, 1994
Painted fine wool shawl,
Contemporary Art Society,
London, England, 1995
Painted silk scarf,
Victoria & Albert Museum,
London, England, 1997

05.08	Heather Belcher

39 Casella Road
London SE14 5QN
England
Tel: +44 171 639 5975

Education
MA Textiles,
Goldsmiths College,
London, England, 1995

Collections/commissions
"Scissors" wall hanging
and "Giant Pullover"
installation,
Crafts Council,
permanent collection,
London, England, 1990

Wall hanging
"Alphabet & Arch Russett".
Hand-painted, stencilled and
hand-printed silk dupion wall
hanging. One-off original.
126 x 236cm (49.5 x 93in)
To commission only

Wall hanging
Series of painted panels
painted with reactive acid
dyes onto spun silk.
260 x 90cm (102.5 x 35.5in)
To commission only

| 05.09 | Neil Bottle | 3 Winterstoke Way
Ramsgate
Kent CT11 8AG
England
Tel: +44 1843 586764
Fax: +44 1843 586764 |

Education
BA (Hons) Printed Textiles,
Middlesex Polytechnic,
England, 1989

Collections/commissions
Victoria & Albert Museum,
permanent collection,
London, England, 1992
Crafts Council,
permanent collection,
London, England, 1994
Commission for scarves and
ties, exclusive designs for
Globe Theatre,
London, England, 1997

Printed fabric
"Diamond design". Hand-dyed, printed and painted silk.
(Fabric samples sold to Christian Lacroix.)
Three samples, each 84 x 24cm (33 x 9.5in)

05.10 | **Kirstine Chaffey**

16a Morley Road
East Twickenham
Middlesex TW1 2HF
England
Tel: +44 181 287 5228

Education
BA (Hons) Printed Textile
Design, Surrey Institute of Art
& Design, Farnham,
England, 1985

Collections/commissions
Hand-printed silk
handkerchiefs, corporate
gifts, Design House,
London, England, 1987
Tie designed for book,
Fabric Painting by Miranda
Innes, Dorling Kindersley,
London, England, 1996
Paintings for office, ties and
scarves as corporate gifts,
Financial Times Information,
London, England, 1997

"MY PIECE IS TRYING TO
RECREATE THE TEXTURE
OF WATER —
THE CONSTANT
MOVEMENT AND CHANGING
SURFACE."

05.11 **Fiona Claydon**

5 Deerswood Close
Caterham
Surrey CR3 6DE
England
Tel: +44 1883 348707
Fax: +44 181 296 8164

Education
BA (Hons) Textile Design,
Surrey Institute of Art &
Design, Farnham,
England, 1996

Screen-printed fabric
Fabric screen-printed with procion print pastes and dye,
using variety of overlaying techniques to produce wide
spectrum of colour. Initial image taken from photographs
scanned onto computer.
300 x 150cm (118 x 59in)
To commission only

Reversible fabric
Wool and silk reversible
fabric.
Repeat size 20 x 20cm
(8 x 8in)
To commission only

05.12 | **Gill Gurney** | 27 Kings Hill
Beech
Alton
Hampshire GU34 4AW
England
Tel: +44 1420 562311
Fax: +44 1420 562311

Education
BA (Hons) Textiles, Surrey
Institute of Art & Design,
Farnham, England, 1997

05.13	Mika Hirosawa

111 Palmerston Road
London SW19 1PB
England
Tel: +44 181 543 8103
or +44 171 681 6010
Fax: +44 181 543 8103

Education
BA (Hons) Textile Design,
Central St Martins
College of Art & Design,
London, England, 1991
MA Textile Design,
Central St Martins
College of Art & Design,
London, England, 1994

Collections/commissions
Fabrics for opera/musical
costumes for designer
Kenichi Nakayama,
Germany, 1995
Fabrics for scarves for
costume for designer
Kenichi Nakayama,
Tokyo, Japan, 1998

Wall hanging
Hand-woven, using silk selvages cut off from industrial silk
weaving (therefore recycled material).
150 x 30cm (59 x 11.75in)
To commission only

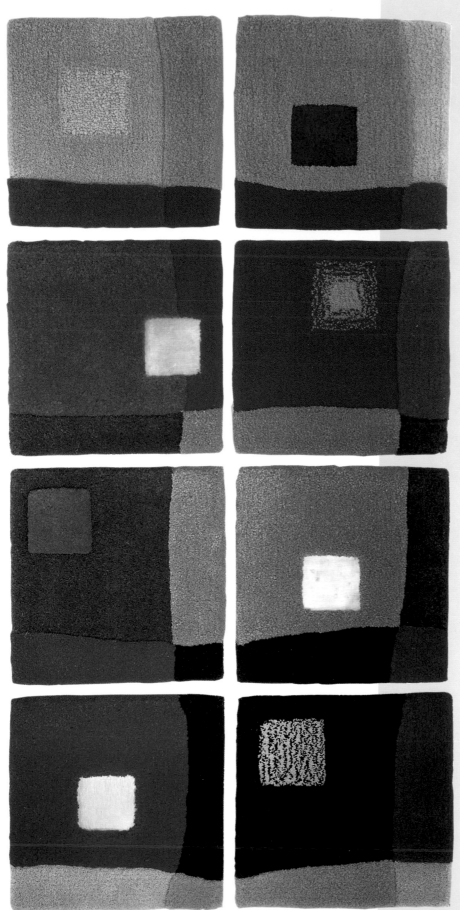

Wall hanging
"Squares in a square". Hand-tufted wall hanging made from 100 per cent pure new wool.
183 x 183cm (72 x 72in)
To commission only

05.14 | **Tracy Hillier**

134 Wynford Road
Islington
London N1 9SW
England
Tel: +44 171 833 2036
Fax: +44 171 837 2999
E-mail:
tracy@thefinerdetail.com
Website:www.thefinerdetail.
com/tracyh

Education
BA (Hons) Carpet Design & Related Textiles, Kidderminster College, England, 1993

Collections/commissions
British Embassy, Dublin, Ireland, 1995–98
Nortel, Harlow, England, 1998
Mondex International, London, England, 1998

05.15 **Zoë Hope**

Unit 7
Cockpit Yard Workshops
Northington Street
London WC1N 2NP
England
Tel: +44 171 916 4437
Fax: +44 171 813 3034

Education
BA Constructed Textiles,
Middlesex University,
England, 1993

Collections/commissions
M.H. de Young Memorial
Museum,
San Francisco, USA, 1996
New York Public Library
shop, New York, USA, 1996
Royal Caribbean
International, Miami, USA,
1997

Wall hanging
"Swimming". Hand-woven silk with preserved fish.
66 x 160cm (26 x 63in)
To commission only

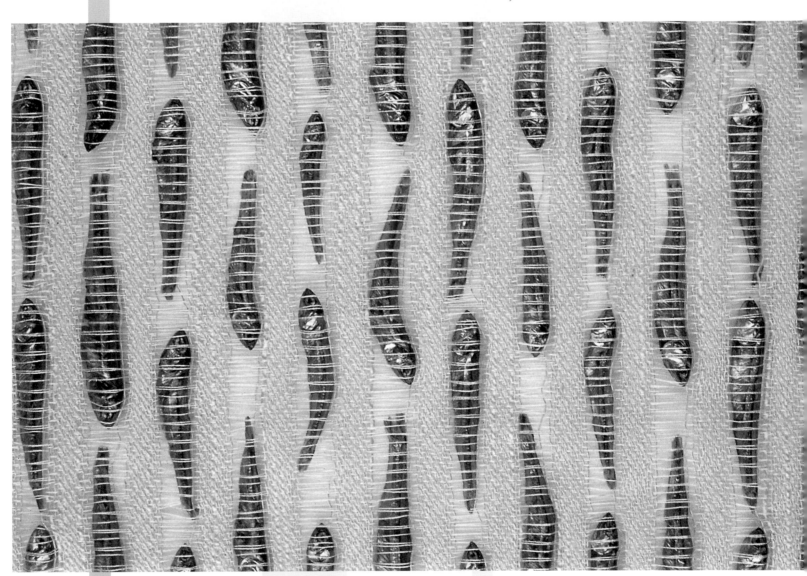

05.16 **Jo Horton**

7 Meadow View
Rolleston on Dove
Burton upon Trent
Staffordshire DE13 9AL
England
Tel: +44 1283 814924

Education

BA (Hons) 3D Design,
Ceramics & Glass,
Birmingham Polytechnic,
England, 1985
MA Textiles/Fashion,
University of Central
England, Birmingham,
England, 1993

Collections/commissions

Wall hanging, Hanley
Museum and Art Gallery,
Stoke-on-Trent, England,
1994
Commissioned co-ordinates,
bedroom cushions for
private client,
Birmingham, England, 1997
Commissioned co-ordinates,
cushion and footstool, for
private client,
Hertfordshire, England,
1998

Cushions

"Snail" collection. Printed and embroidered (machine- and
hand-stitched) grounds for interior use. All surfaces
individually dyed and manipulated, with washaway, glass,
button-tuft or tassel additions.
Bolster 50 x dia. 20cm (19.5 x 8in)
Square cushion 38 x 38cm (15 x 15in)
To commission only

"MY INTENTIONS ARE TO
CREATE INTRIGUING AND
SENSITIVELY MANIPULATED
SURFACES, FOUNDED IN THE
INSPIRATION OF WILDLIFE
AND RELATED HABITS."

05.17	Michelle House

20 Wray House
Streatham Hill
London SW2 4AR
England
Tel: +44 181 674 9026
Fax: +44 181 501 9309

Education
BA (Hons) Textiles,
Goldsmiths College,
London, England, 1992

Collection/commissions
Banner designs for
Canary Wharf Limited,
London, England, 1997
Textile commission for
Hove Polyclinic,
South Downs NHS Trust,
Sussex, England, 1997–98

Wall hanging
Hand-painted and printed
canvas using direct dyes and
pigment discharge, with
photographic and paper
stencils.
100 x 170cm (39.5 x 67in)
To commission only

05.18 | Rachael Howard

14 Groombridge Road
Hackney
London E9 7DP
England
Tel: +44 181 986 9889
Fax: +44 181 986 9889
E-mail: raehoward@aol.com

Education
MA (RCA) Embroidery,
Royal College of Art,
London, England, 1992

Collections/commissions
Wall hanging for office
entrance,
North-West Arts Board,
Manchester, England, 1996
Wall hanging, Crafts Council,
permanent collection,
London, England, 1996
Permanent collection based
on clothes recycling,
Museum of Science and
Industry, Manchester,
England, 1997

Wall hanging
"Indian Embroidery Factory". Screen-printed drawings,
various appliquéd fabrics and machine embroidery. Base
fabric of cambric cotton.
145 x 225cm (57 x 88in)
To commission only

"THERE ARE SO MANY NEW FABRICS, TECHNIQUES AND PRINT MEDIA AVAILABLE TODAY IN A BROAD SECTION OF THE TEXTILE INDUSTRY; SOME OF THESE NEED TO BE PUT TO INNOVATIVE USE IN MODERN CONTEMPORARY INTERIORS."

05.19	Ilex Textile Design

Holly Reynolds
25 Kirkway
Broadstone
Dorset BH18 8ED
England
Tel: +44 1202 696857
Fax: +44 1202 696857

Education
BA (Hons) Printed Textile
Design, Loughborough
College of Art & Design,
England, 1997

Collections/commissions
3m (10ft) hanging for
archives and promotion of
college, Loughborough
College of Art & Design,
England, 1997

Furnishing fabrics
Silk/viscose velvet discharge screen-printed samples.
36 x 36cm (14 x 14in)
To commission only

Printed fabrics, upholstered couch and stools
Photographic silkscreen-printed fruit and flower imagery
printed onto silk, velvet, chiffon and organza.
Fabrics 91.5-137cm wide (36-54in)
Couch 200 x 250cm (78.5 x 98.5in)
Stools height 55cm (21.5in)
To commission only

05.20	Jan Milne Textile Design

Jan Milne
Unit 19, Govan Workspace
Six Harmony Row
Govan
Glasgow G51 3BA
Scotland
Tel: +44 141 445 5554
Fax: +44 141 445 5554

Education
BA (Hons) Printed Textile
Design,
Glasgow School of Art,
Scotland, 1994

Collections/commissions
Upholstery fabric for Genki
sushi bar, Fifth Avenue,
New York, USA, 1997
350m (1138ft) of fabric
printed for bedroom interior
of beach house in
Nassau, Bahamas, 1998
Three designs sold for a
range of plastic products,
Koziol, Frankfurt,
Germany, 1998

Throw and cushion
"Aqua Dot". Hand-made throw/bedspread and co-ordinated
cushions. White cotton velvet, dyed and printed by hand.
Throw 250 x 165cm (98.5 x 65in)
Cushions 50 x 50cm (19.5 x 19.5in)
To commission only

Window screen
Laminated, coated and surface-treated.
Synthetic meshes and open wovens.
200 x 65cm (78.75 x 25.5in)
To commission only

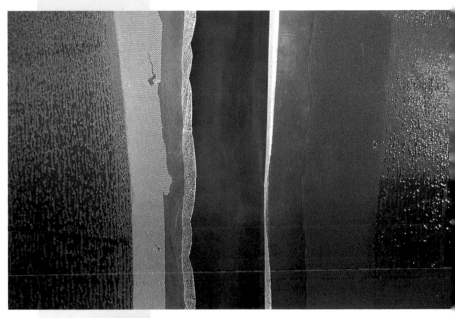

05.21	Jane Keith Designs	**Jane Keith**

Inverforth Studios
50 Laverockbank Road
Trinity
Edinburgh EH5 3BZ
Scotland
Tel: +44 131 552 8198
Fax: +44 131 226 3042

Education
BDes (Hons) Printed Textiles,
Duncan of Jordanstone
College of Art,
Dundee, Scotland, 1995

Collections/commissions
Liberty Brand Products,
illustrations for Liberty
Recipe Book, 1996
Banner for Science Building
entrance, in collaboration
with Open Eye Gallery,
Edinburgh, Scotland, 1997

05.22	Emma Jeffs	16 Cambridge Drive

Lee
London SE12 8AJ
England
Tel: +44 181 852 2802
Fax: +44 181 265 4529

Education
BA (Hons) Fashion Textiles,
University of the West of
England, Bristol, England,
1995
MA Fashion, Textiles &
Surface Design,
University of Central
England, Birmingham,
England, 1998

Collections/commissions
Six sculptural fabric pieces,
"The edge between art and
fashion", Chapel Street
Gallery, Bath, England, 1997
New English PR, two
sculptural hats, brochure for
McNaughtons Paper
Company, Birmingham,
England, 1997
Fabric for catwalk installation
for live interactive fashion
event, Central England
Generation Show,
The Custard Factory,
Birmingham, England, 1998

Interior textile/hanging
"Warp Only Brick". Woven wool and cotton construction fabric. Decorated with *devoré*, burn-out technique to expose integral warp structure.
241 x 89cm (95 x 35in)
To commission only

05.23 | **Gilian Little**

Studio 39
Cornwell House
21 Clerkenwell Green
London EC1R 0DE
England
Tel: +44 181 673 6845
Fax: +44 171 250 0297

Education
MA (RCA) Woven Textiles,
Royal College of Art,
London, England, 1993

Collections/commissions
Victoria & Albert Museum,
permanent collection,
London, England, 1997
Crafts Council,
permanent collection,
London, England, 1998

05.24 **Natasha Kerr**

Studio W11
Cockpit Yard Workshops
Northington Street
London WC1N 2NP
England
Tel: +44 171 916 4640
Fax: +44 171 916 4640

Education
BA (Hons) Fashion Textiles
with Business,
Brighton University,
England, 1992

Collections/commissions
Hangings for the foyer of
Gefinor Investment Bank,
New York, USA, 1997
Hangings for Caribbean
cruise liner *Enchantment of
the Seas*,
Royal Caribbean
International,
Miami, USA, 1997
Hangings for
Rudding House Hotel,
Yorkshire, England, 1997

Framed textile piece
"Who is the Naked Lady?". Hand-painted and hand-stitched
antique linen. Flocked and screen-printed areas.
150 x 130cm (60 x 52in)
To commission only

Wall hanging
"Basking Aphrodite". Machine-stitched. Threads of cotton,
rayon, metallic, silk.
33 x 44cm (13 x 17.25in)
*To commission only. Framed pieces available from the studio,
by appointment*

05.25 **Alice Kettle**

12 Arthur Road
Winchester
Hampshire SO23 7EA
England
Fax: +44 1962 864727

Education
BA Fine Art,
Reading University,
England, 1984
Postgraduate Diploma in
Textile Art,
Special Commendation,
Goldsmiths College,
London, England, 1986

Collections/commissions
"Stretching Figure",
Crafts Council,
permanent collection,
London, England, 1990
"Glimpses of India", on
board *MV Oriana*,
P&O Cruises, 1994–95
"In Camera", High Court,
Lawnmarket, Edinburgh,
Scotland, 1996–97

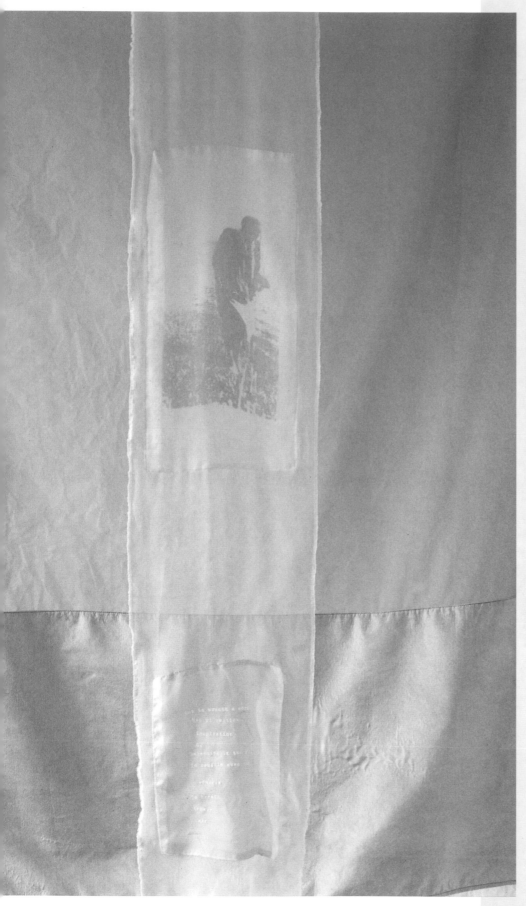

05.26 **Stéphanie Malossane** Unit 1
Omnibus Workspace
39–41 North Road
London N7 9DP
England
Tel: +44 171 609 1137
Fax: +44 171 609 1137

Education
BTS Textile Design and
Printing, Ecole Superieure
des Arts Appliqués Dupérré,
Paris, France, 1991
MA Textile Design,
Central St Martins College of
Art & Design,
London, England, 1993

Collections/commissions
"Anthropologie" store display
textile window panels and
display fabric, Wayne,
Pennsylvania, Washington,
DC, Westport, Connecticut,
Newport Beach, California,
Santa Monica, California and
New York, USA, 1992–96
"Tuscan Square" decorative
wall hangings and display
fabric, The Rockefeller
Centre, New York, USA, 1997
Textile panels for columns in
hotel lobby, Doral Inn,
New York, USA, 1998

Window panels
"To Breathe" (front panel).
100 per cent silk with screen-
printed, hand-painted and
hand-marked appliqués.
*35 x 189cm
(13.75 x 74.75in)
In production*

"Brume" (back panel).
Made from 100 per cent
nylon and silk trimming.
*137 x 245cm (54 x 96.5in)
In production*

05.27 **Kumi Middleton**

36 Tyler Way
Thrapston
Kettering
Northamptonshire
NN14 4UE
England
Tel: +44 1832 735836

Education
BA (Hons) Textile Design,
Central St Martins College of
Art & Design,
London, England, 1995

Collections/commissions
Contemporary Applied Arts,
London, England, 1997

Wall hanging
Wool, monofilament,
feathers, organza, metal,
knitted, embroidered,
machine-quilted.
*40 x 200cm
(15.75 x 78.75in)
To commission only*

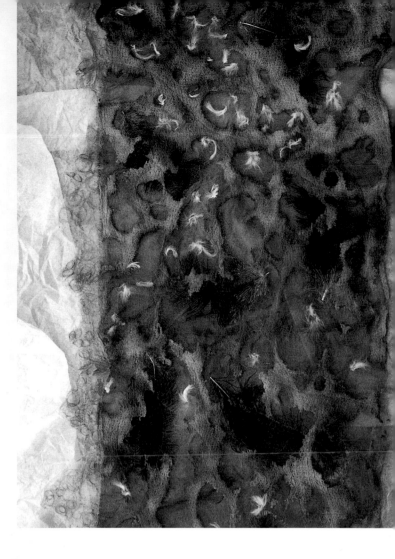

Wall hanging
"Aboont Spoons". Dyed,
screen-printed, hand-painted
and devoré silk velvet.
*60 x 100cm (23.5 x 39.5in)
To commission only*

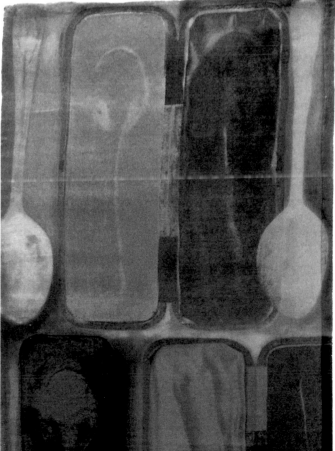

05.28 **Joanna Kinnersly-Taylor
Fine Art Printed Textiles**

Joanna Kinnersly-Taylor
2nd Floor
Renfrew Chambers
20 Renfrew Street
Glasgow G2 3BW
Scotland
Tel: +44 141 332 4401
Fax: +44 141 332 4401

Education
BA (Hons) Printed Textiles,
West Surrey Institute of Art &
Design, Farnham, England,
1988
MA Design, Glasgow School
of Art, Scotland, 1994

Collections/commissions
Altar diptych,
Cambridge City
Crematorium,
England, 1991
Series of 16 wall hangings
and panels, Ayr Hospital,
Scotland, 1995
Seven wall hangings and
wool rug, Innovation Centre,
West Lakes Science &
Technology Park,
Cumbria, England, 1998

Textile art piece
"Heat 4". Hand-dyed and
woven using linen and
wool fibres.
35 x 35 x 5cm (14 x 14 x 2in)
To commission only

Textile art piece
"Orange and Purple
Space 1". Hand-dyed and
woven on upright dobby
loom, using rayon, cotton
and silk fibres.
40 x 50 x 5cm
(15.5 x 19.5 x 2in)
To commission only

05.29	Ptolemy Mann	Flat 8

9 Stamford Hill
Stoke Newington
London N16 5TU
England
Tel: +44 181 809 4218

Education
BA Textile Design,
Central St Martins College of
Art & Design,
London, England, 1995
MA (RCA) Constructed
Textiles, Royal College of Art,
London, England, 1997

Collections/commissions
"Seven Countries"
commission for
KPMG Accountants,
London, England, 1996
"Gate House" commission
for SLC Asset Management,
London, England, 1997
Woven art pieces for
Midnight Transfer,
film post-production facility,
London, England, 1997

"MY AIM IS TO CREATE MODERN,
WOVEN, TEXTILE ART PIECES
THAT MOVE IN A DIFFERENT DIRECTION
FROM TAPESTRY OR FIBRE ART —
CLEAN, STRETCHED
CANVASES THAT FUNCTION
IN A COLLABORATIVE WAY WITH
ARCHITECTURE, USING COLOUR
AND LINE TO ENHANCE A PUBLIC OR
DOMESTIC SPACE."

05.30 | Neil Musson

Walnut Cottage
East Dean
Salisbury
Wiltshire SP5 1HJ
England
Tel: +44 1794 340586
(voicemail)
or +44 402 107679 (mobile)

Education
BA (Hons) Woven Textiles,
Surrey Institute of Art &
Design, Farnham, England,
1994
MA (RCA) Constructed
Textiles, Royal College of Art,
London, England, 1996

Collections/commissions
Illuminating woven wire,
Philip Treacy,
London, England, and
New York, USA, 1997
Wire hangings for interiors,
Lady Willoughby de Broke,
Oxfordshire, England, 1997
Sheer fabrics,
Osborne & Little,
London, England, 1997

"MY DESIGNS PUT CONSIDERABLE EMPHASIS ON A PROCESS OF EDITING — A PROCESS WHICH I BELIEVE TYPIFIES CONTEMPORARY DESIGN. ALL SUPERFLUOUS MARKS ARE REMOVED, LEAVING A SIMPLIFIED, HARMONIOUS FORM. ORNAMENTATION HAS BEEN ABSORBED INTO STRUCTURE."

Woven hanging
Woven wire hanging/screen. Hand-woven insulated wire
using heat-bonding to fix structure. Size according to client's
requirements.
Detail 20 x 30cm (8 x 11.75in)
To commission only

Passementerie
Silk gimp braid (foreground) and silk cut fringe (background), trellised with fine cords and wooden beads.
Gimp 5cm (2in),
Fringe 13cm (5.25in)
To commission only

Passementerie
Braid with fine cords and beads, silk and cotton; silk trellis gimp braid in background.
Braid 10.5cm (4.25in), trellis gimp 9cm (3.5in)
To commission only

05.31	Frances Soubeyran

12 Atlas Mews
Ramsgate Street
London E8 2NE
England
Tel: +44 171 241 1064
Fax: +44 171 241 1064

Education
BA (Hons) Constructed Textiles,
Middlesex Polytechnic,
England, 1981

Collections/commissions
Silk/linen fringe for wall hangings, private chapel,
Wolvesey Palace,
Winchester, England, 1994
Silk striped fringes, Boodles,
St. James' salon,
London, England, 1996
Collection of trimmings for private residence, including tie-backs in cotton with gilded elements,
incorporating glass and silk,
London, England, 1997–98

Wall hanging
Waxed-silk wall hanging.
Design etched through wax
and then dyed with natural
pigments, K salt and indigo.
35 x 135cm (13.75 x 53in)
To commission only

"I DRAW UPON THE
COLOUR, IMAGERY
AND VISUAL
QUALITY OF THE DIFFERENT
ENVIRONMENTS
WHICH I HAVE VISITED
DURING MY
RECENT TRAVELS.
THIS FORMS AN
IMPORTANT THEME
IN MY WORK, USING
TRADITIONAL COLOUR
AND CRAFT
AND TRANSLATING
THEM INTO A
MODERN IDIOM."

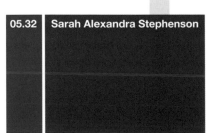

| 05.32 | **Sarah Alexandra Stephenson** | 26a Cheshire Street |

26a Cheshire Street
London E2 6EH
England
Tel:+44 171 613 2163
Fax:+44 171 613 2163

Education
BA (Hons) Textiles, Surrey
Institute of Art & Design,
Farnham, England, 1997

**Karina Holmes and
June Swindell**
2.04 Oxo Tower Wharf
Bargehouse Street
London SE1 9PH
England
Tel: +44 171 593 0007
Fax: +44 171 593 0007

Education
Karina Holmes — BA (Hons)
Textile Design,
University of Leeds,
England, 1989
MA (RCA) Knitted Textiles,
Royal College of Art,
London, England, 1992
June Swindell — BA (Hons)
Fashion and Textiles,
Liverpool Polytechnic,
England, 1993
MA Woven Textiles,
Nottingham Trent University,
England, 1995

Collections/commissions
Collection of cushions and
throws, Harrods,
London, England, 1997
Panoramic window at
Manhattan Lofts,
South Bank,
London, England, 1998
Installation at
The Fitch Gallery,
Commonwealth House,
London, England, 1998

Woven blind
"Beam". Hand-woven
monofilament cotton,
incorporating stainless-steel
rods for form. Window
space used by blind as light
source, fluorescent filaments
emitting night-time glow, yet
simple, modern monotones
during day.
*100 x 200cm
(39.5 x 78.75in)
To commission only*

Stool
"Squigee Pouf". Upholstered with rubberised sides and coloured cotton top. Available in two sizes.
Small 30 x dia. 45cm (12 x 17.75in)
Large 44 x dia. 45cm (17.25 x 17.75in)
To commission only

05.34	Squigee Textile Design

Neil Fullerton and Natasha Marshall
Number 7
149 Crown Road South
Glasgow G12 9DP
Scotland
Tel: +44 141 334 0661
Fax: +44 141 341 0532
E-mail: squigee@cqm.co.uk

Education
Neil Fullerton — BA (Hons) Graphic Design, Glasgow School of Art, Scotland, 1994
Postgraduate Diploma, Electronic Imaging, Duncan of Jordanstone College, Dundee, Scotland, 1996
Natasha Marshall — BA (Hons) Printed & Knitted Textiles, Glasgow School of Art, Scotland, 1996

Collections/commissions
Contract fabrics, Malmaison Hotel Group, Manchester, England, and Glasgow, Scotland, 1998
Fabrics for Macbeth ladies collection, Glasgow, Scotland, 1998

Sophie Williams
91 Lausanne Road
London SE15 2HY
England
Tel: +44 171 639 7524
or +44 181 291 6712
Fax: +44 171 639 7524
or +44 181 291 6712

Education
BA (Hons) Textiles/Fashion,
Middlesex University,
England, 1992

Collections/commissions
Six one-off pieces,
British Gas headquarters,
London, England, 1997
Interior fabrics, including
curtains and cushions,
private commission,
London, England, 1998
Own-label Autumn fashion
collection, including coats,
jackets, tunics, trousers and
one-off pieces to order,
London, England, 1998

Silk hanging
183 x 122cm (72 x 48in)
To commission only

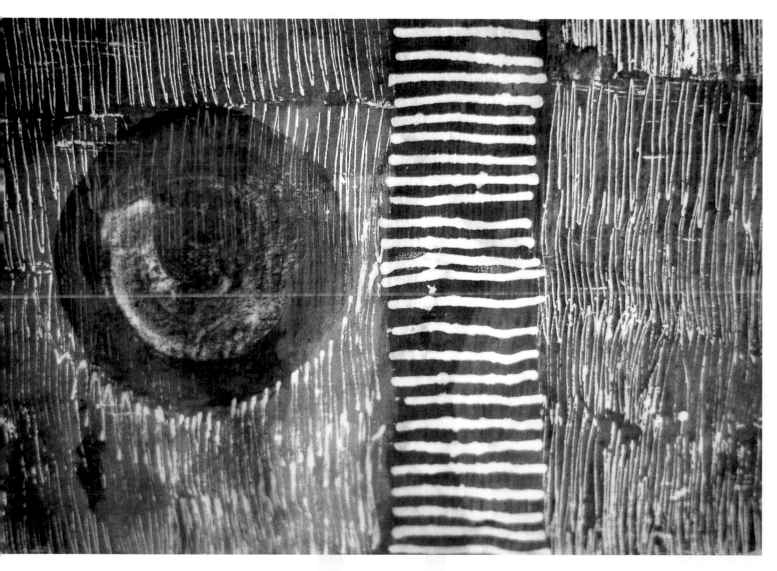

05.36 **Usha**

Usha Mahenthiralingam
House of Hearts
15 Lord Nelson Street
Sneinton
Nottingham NG2 4FA
England
Tel: +44 115 911 8353

Education
BA (Hons) Printed Textiles,
Loughborough College of Art
& Design, England, 1985

Collections/commissions
Four prints, Rampton Prison,
England, 1993
Banners, "Gardens in the
sky", Belgrave Library,
Leicester, England, 1994
Design of crèche/expressive
arts room,
Doncaster Community Arts,
Doncaster, England, 1998

Wall hanging
"Sea Sky over Golden
Sand". Screen-printed on
cotton.
61 x 137cm (24 x 54in)
To commission only

Tablecloth
Linen cloth appliquéd and
machine-embroidered.
150 x 150cm (59 x 59in)
To commission only

05.38 | **Lisa Vaughan** | Unit 258
Clerkenwell Workshops
27–31 Clerkenwell Close
London EC1R 0AT
England
Tel: +44 171 250 0085
Fax: +44 171 250 0085

Education
HND Textile Design,
Derbyshire College,
Derby, England, 1989
MA (RCA) Textile Design,
Royal College of Art,
London, England, 1992

Collections/commissions
Blankets, cushions and
interior accessories for the
home of Tricia Guild,
Designers Guild,
London, England, 1997
Blinds and cushions for the
home of Lesley Knox,
Sussex, England, 1997

Furnishing textiles
"Stars". 100 per cent
synthetic fabric, patterned by
CO_2 photon laser beams to
obtain "laserlace".
Width 150 x min 100cm
(59 x min. 39.5in)
To commission only

05.37 | **The Cloth Clinic** | **Janet Stoyel**
The Old Rectory
Sheldon
near Honiton
Devon EX14 0QU
England
Tel: +44 1404 841350
Fax: +44 1404 841718

Education
BA (Hons) Constructed
Textiles,
University of Central
England,
Birmingham, England, 1992
MPhil (RCA) Textiles,
Royal College of Art,
London, England, 1994

Collections/commissions
Collection of leather
products, Donna Karan,
worldwide, 1997
Collection of ultralace,
Philip Treacy, three seasons,
London, England, 1997–98
Laserlace collections,
Paloma Picasso,
worldwide, 1998

Printed fabric
"Funky Palette". 3-colour pigment print onto cotton.
Repeat size 78 x 136cm (30.75 x 53.75in)
In production

Printed fabric
"Fini Tribe". 18-colour print, procion dye onto cotton velvet.
Repeat size 90 x 120cm (35.5 x 47.25in)
In production

05.39	Timorous Beasties

Alistair McAuley and Paul Simmons
7 Craigend Place
Glasgow G13 2UN
Scotland
Tel: +44 141 959 3331
Fax: +44 141 959 8880
E-mail:
info@timorousbeasties.
demon.co.uk
Website:
www.timorousbeasties.
demon.co.uk

Education
Alistair McAuley —
BA (Hons) Printed Textiles,
Glasgow School of Art,
Scotland, 1988
Postgraduate Diploma
Printed Textiles,
Glasgow School of Art,
Scotland, 1989
Paul Simmons — BA (Hons)
Printed Textiles,
Glasgow School of Art,
Scotland, 1988
MA (RCA) Printed Textiles,
Royal College of Art,
London, England, 1990

Collections/commissions
Cooper-Hewitt National
Design Museum,
permanent collection,
New York, USA, 1992
Victoria & Albert Museum,
permanent collection,
London, England, 1993
Gallery of Modern Art,
permanent collection,
Glasgow, Scotland, 1995

05.40 | **Kate Tayler** | Top Floor
16 Portland Street
Kingsdown
Bristol
Avon BS2 8HL
England
Tel: +44 117 942 4842

Education
BA (Hons) Textile Design,
Chelsea College of Art and
Design, London, England,
1997

Hanging textile
Velvet pile weaving.
91 x 34cm (35.75 x 13.5in)
To commission only

| 05.41 | Prue Jessop |

43b Mansfield Road
London NW3 2JE
England
Tel: +44 171 485 0860
Fax: +44 171 209 5185
E-mail: p.jessop@rca.ac.uk

Education
MA Textile Design,
Winchester School of Art,
England, 1994
MPhil (RCA) Constructed
Textiles,
Royal College of Art,
London, England, 1998

Wall hanging
Organzine and raw silk warps. Linen, nylon, paper, polyester,
tin and enamel-coated copper wire weft. Power-woven
textiles on turn-of-the-century shuttle looms at Whitchurch
Silk Mill, Hampshire, England. Commissioned by The
Worshipful Company of Weavers, London, England, 1998.
142 x 108cm (56 x 42.5in)
To commission only

Tablecloths
"Flanders". Woven cotton, double-cloth tablecloth fabric.
165 x 165cm (65 x 65in)
In production

| 05.42 | Wallace Sewell | **Harriet Wallace-Jones and Emma Sewell** |

Unit 168
Clerkenwell Workshops
27–31 Clerkenwell Close
London EC1R 0AT
England
Tel: +44 171 251 2143
Fax: +44 171 251 2143

Education
Harriet Wallace-Jones and
Emma Sewell — BA (Hons)
Textile Design,
Central St Martins College
of Art & Design,
London, England, 1988
MA (RCA) Woven Textiles,
Royal College of Art,
London, England, 1990

Collections/commissions
Design and production of
bespoke curtain for concert
hall, The Anvil, Basingstoke,
England, 1994
Development and production
of new fabric to replicate
antique Uzbekistan "camel
blanket", London, England,
1996–97
Crafts Council,
permanent collection,
London, England, 1998

| 05.43 | Christine Wallace | Weavers |

Weare Street
Capel
Surrey RH5 5HY
England
Tel: +44 1306 711205

Education
BA (Hons) Textiles,
Surrey Institute of Art
& Design, Farnham,
England, 1997

Collections/commissions
"Not Garden", woven
hanging for St Michael's
Hospital, Warwick,
England, 1995
Replica seat for 19th-century
Shaker chair, private
collection, Surrey,
England, 1996

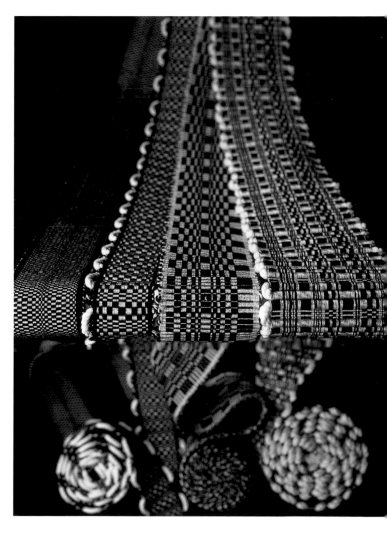

Braids
Hand-woven, warp-faced braids in silk and wool, for
interior finishes. Winner of The Society of Designer Craftsmen
Award, 1998.
5–10cm (2–4in)
To commission only

06Metalwork

Introduction
Peta Levi

In the introduction to this book, I described how a group of silversmiths who graduated from the Royal College of Art in the 1950s opened new vistas for British silversmiths. Today, designers continue to enjoy using silver to create contemporary designs. Silversmiths work in many different ways, from someone such as Richard Fox, who supplies cost-effective, simple, well-designed silverware to retailers (but also undertakes one-off commissions), to Rod Kelly, a great craftsman in the spirit of the Arts and Crafts Movement, who only makes one-off pieces and is one of the leaders in chased silver and inlaid gold work (see page 176).

There is a growing interest in combining silver with other materials. Rebecca de Quin's example of a silver and glass water set (see page 182) demonstrates this trend of making silver accessible to many people who hanker after owning objects which include such a beautiful material.

The new generation of silversmiths includes Tanya Mila Griebel, Richardson & Ottewill, Justine Huntley and David Clarke – all of them makers of silver which people can use and enjoy in their homes. David Clarke, whose work is illustrated on page 170, is a good example of a silversmith who has created an entirely new and practical idea – in his case, a not exorbitantly expensive table centrepiece for holding fruit or flowers. Another new idea is a pair of contact lens holders with different coloured stones to differentiate between left and right lenses, made by Richardson & Ottewill. A further instance of how many young silversmiths are designing products for today's living styles is the growing interest in creating utensils for different cuisines, particularly Japanese and Chinese – you will see numerous examples in this book.

"IN BRITAIN THE INCREASE IN THE NUMBER OF PEOPLE WHO ARE COMMISSIONING METALWORKERS TO DESIGN AND MAKE STAIRCASES, BALUSTRADES GARDEN GATES AND OTHER ARTEFACTS IS STRIKING."

However, in the last 20 years significant developments have also taken place in those crafts that use other important metals. In 1979 Camberwell School of Art became the first in Britain to include ironsmithing in its BA course. The next year, 28-year-old Giuseppe Lund formed a small group of experimental blacksmiths at Coalbrookdale in Shropshire's Ironbridge Gorge, at the invitation of Dr Neil Cossons, then Director of the Ironbridge Gorge Museum. Ironbridge, where iron had been worked for hundreds of years, was an appropriate place for the birth of a new iron age. Giuseppe introduced a breath of fresh air into the world of traditional ironwork. Aware of the high quality of contemporary ironwork on the Continent, he was determined to alter the dismissive view of British ironwork held by Continental cognoscenti.

In the same year, 1980, the Crafts Council organised an international conference on "Forging Iron" at the Ironbridge Gorge Museum. This led to a growing interest in forging iron and other metals for a wide variety of products, from jewellery to architectural work such as shop fronts, staircases, gates, furniture and lighting. In some cases, the fluidity of iron has often led to over-elaborate decoration and a lack of restraint in form and design, which is a possible explanation for the lack of examples in this book of ironwork that represents this movement. However, iron and metal have become popular media for young British designers, and I hope that the next edition of this book will contain more examples.

One giant, and totally individual, designer working in metal is Ron Arad. Ron, who trained as an artist and architect, straddles the two worlds of one-off design and design for manufacture, creating original and innovative one-off pieces of furniture at the same time as designing for international furniture manufacturers and undertaking major architectural projects. His influence has been far-reaching and inspirational.

Another catalyst for change has been The Worshipful Company of Pewterers. One of the City of London's ancient livery companies, for the last 12 years it has positively encouraged colleges and universities to be involved with creating contemporary designs for pewter, by initiating an active educational programme for relevant courses, by providing sponsorship of the material for students, and by making awards. This dedicated involvement is reaping its reward. The Company is currently assembling a Millennium Collection of contemporary pewter, which will include an innovative and tactile paperknife by Alan Pickersgill (see page 171).

In Britain the increase in the number of people who are commissioning metalworkers to design and make staircases, balustrades, garden gates and other artefacts is striking. This is a fertile time for metalwork. I predict exciting developments for this craft in the next millennium.

Detail from a vase by Alex Brogden (see page 165)

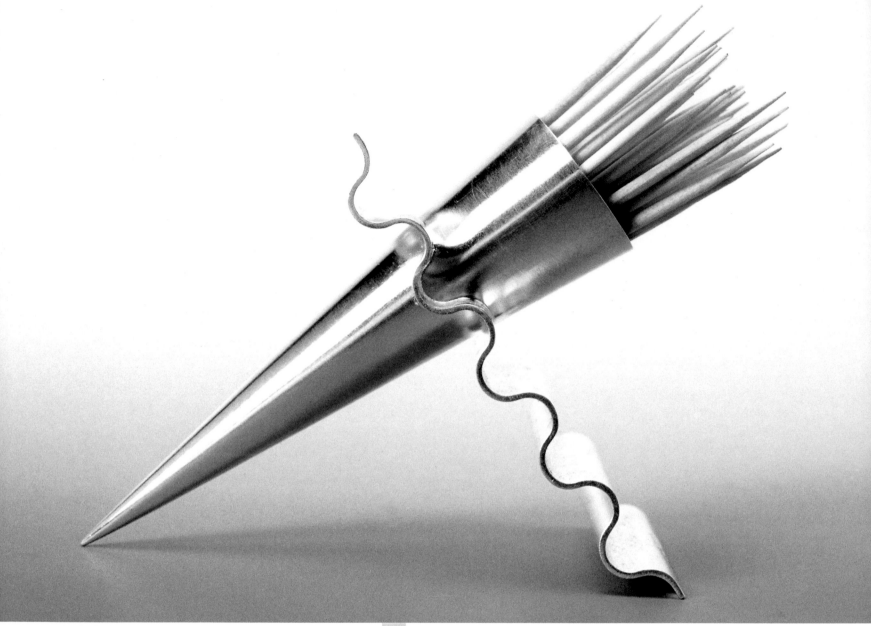

Toothpick holder
Silver-cone and corrugated silver. Corrugation made by
specially designed tool.
7.5cm (3in)
To commission only

06.01 | **Linda Robertson**

2 Croc-an-Raer
Ettrick Bay
North Bute
Rothesay
Isle of Bute PA20 0QT
Scotland
Tel: +44 1700 504059

Education
BA (Hons) Design
(Silversmithing & Jewellery),
Glasgow School of Art,
Scotland, 1997

"I FEEL I HAVE ONLY SCRATCHED
THE SURFACE, BOTH IN THE
NUMBER OF MATERIALS
THAT I USE AND IN THE WAY
I HAVE USED THEM."

06.02 | **Deborah Jane Schlamp**

30 Higgins House
Colville Estate
Whitmore Road
Hoxton
London N1 5PR
England
Tel: +44 171 739 7715

Education
BA (Hons) 3D Design (Metal),
Middlesex University,
England, 1997

Lemon and tangerine holder
Forged-steel bars spot-welded together for holding lemons
and tangerines.
109 x 18 x 13.5cm (43 x 7 x 5.25in)
To commission only

Japanese dinner set
Set dinner for formal occasions or take-away meals. Thrown stoneware, brass and forged silver.
25 x 18cm (9.75 x 7in)
To commission only

| 06.03 | **Pete Stevens** | 35 Water Lane |

Melbourn
Cambridgeshire SG8 6AY
England
Tel: +44 1763 261858
Website:
www.candidarts.com

Education
BA (Hons) Visual Arts,
Camberwell College of Art,
London, England, 1997

Vase/metal container
"Hen." Prefabricated steel, glass and sieve (detachable).
Vase 18 x dia. 7cm (7 x 2.75in)
Sieve 14 x 10 x dia. 22cm (5.5 x 4 x 8.5in)
Prototype

| 06.04 | **Hans Stofer** | 81 Boundaries Road |

London SW12 8HA
England
Tel: +44 181 673 2928
Fax: +44 181 673 2928

Education
Diploma Mechanical
Engineering,
Brown Boveri College,
Baden, Switzerland, 1976
MA Product Design, Höhere
Schule für Gestaltung,
Zürich, Switzerland, 1984

Collections/commissions
Crafts Council,
permanent collection,
London, England, 1993
Contemporary Art Society,
permanent collection,
London, England, 1993
Galèrie Marzee, Nijmegen,
The Netherlands, 1997

Oil and vinegar set
Sterling silver and glass, using spinning, casting and
fabrication techniques.
25 x dia. 25cm (10 x 10in)
In production

06.05 | William Warren

34 Cambria Road
Camberwell
London SE5 9AE
England
Tel: +44 171 733 0538
Fax: +44 171 703 6137

Education
BDes Design, Liverpool
Institute of Higher Education,
England, 1995
MA (RCA) Silversmithing,
Royal College of Art,
London, England, 1997

Collections/commissions
Commissioned by The
Worshipful Company of
Goldsmiths for the Annual
Silver Grant, Liverpool,
England, 1995
Commissioned to design
and make the "Young
Jazz Musician of the Year"
trophy, London, England,
1996
"Renaissance" collection and
competition, Aylesford
Newsprint, Kent, England,
1996-97

"EVOLUTION HAS
PROVEN ITSELF
TO BE THE BEST DESIGNER OF
PURE FUNCTION,
SO IT IS THE JOB
OF THE INDIVIDUAL
DESIGNER-MAKER TO ADD
SOMETHING BEYOND
FUNCTION,
A PERSONALITY
THAT PROVOKES THOUGHT."

06.06 | **Kelvin Birk** | 45 Bonham Road
Brixton
London SW2 5HN
England
Tel: +44 171 274 0453

Education
MA Silversmithing &
Jewellery,
London Guildhall University,
England, 1997

Collections/commissions
Altar set, Protestant church,
Tainan, Taiwan, 1998

Wine pitcher
Raised in sterling silver with
coloured concrete inlaid in
handle.
Height 30cm (11.75in)
To commission only

Vase
"Wave Vase." Fine silver
formed onto hand-
carved wax.
Height 38cm (15in)
To commission only

"SILVER CAN BE A
SUPER-FINE
MODELLING MATERIAL
THAT REFLECTS LIGHT
IN A SPECIAL WAY.
I TRY TO ABSTRACT THE
ESSENCE OF NATURAL
GEOMETRY."

06.07 **Alex Brogden**

c/o The Crafts Council
44a Pentonville Road
London N1 9BY
England
Tel: +44 114 230 7708
Fax: +44 114 230 9634

Education
MA (RCA) Silversmithing,
Royal College of Art,
London, England, 1986

Collections/commissions
Rosewater Dish,
Corpus Christi College,
Cambridge, England, 1992
Candelabra, The Silver Trust,
10 Downing Street,
London, England, 1992
Lord Tombs Rosewater Dish,
The Worshipful Company
of Goldsmiths, London,
England, 1996

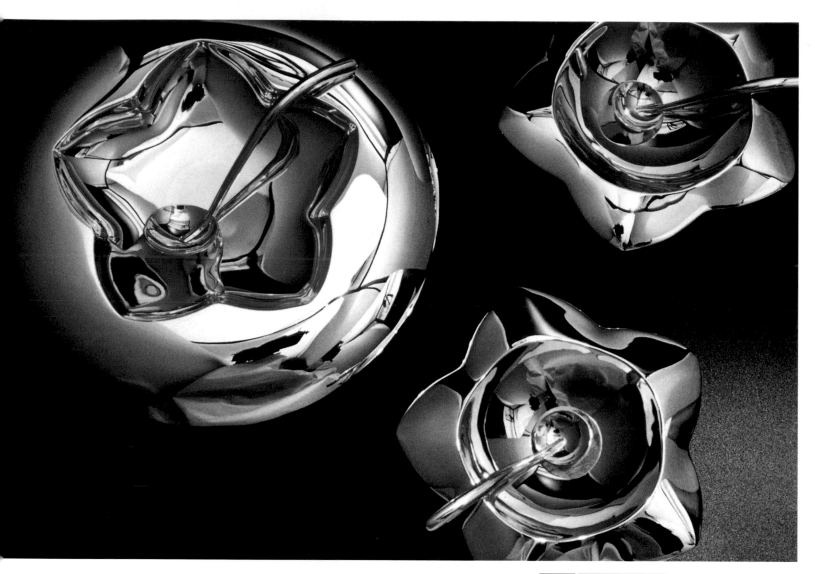

Table salts and spoons
"Star" salts and relish bowl in sterling silver and parcel gilt,
press-formed from sheet and fabricated.
Salts dia. 9cm (3.5in)
Relish bowl dia. 13.5cm (5.25in)
In production

| 06.08 | David Bromilow | Studio 2F
Cockpit Arts
Northington Street
London WC1N 2NP
England
Tel: +44 171 419 5674
Fax: +44 171 916 2455

Education
BA (Hons) Design,
Duncan of Jordanstone
College of Art, Dundee,
Scotland, 1991

Collections/commissions
Aberdeen Art Gallery
collection, Scotland, 1995
The Millennium Canteen
collection, Sheffield City
Council, England, 1997
Commission,
P&O Makower Trust,
Crafts Council,
permanent collection,
London, England, 1998

06.09 | Simon Burns

314 Brithweunydd Road
Tonypandy
Mid Glamorgan CF40 2NY
Wales
Tel: +44 1443 440449
or +44 1443 423493

Education
BA (Hons) 3D Design (Wood,
Metal, Ceramics & Glass),
Manchester Metropolitan
University, England, 1996

**Salt, pepper and
mustard set**
Spun and raised silver with
blown glass inlay, decoration
turned, chased and
coloured.
Salt and pepper pots
18.5 x dia. 2.5cm
(7.25 x 1in)
Mustard dish
10 x dia. 13.5cm
(4 x 5.25in)
To commission only

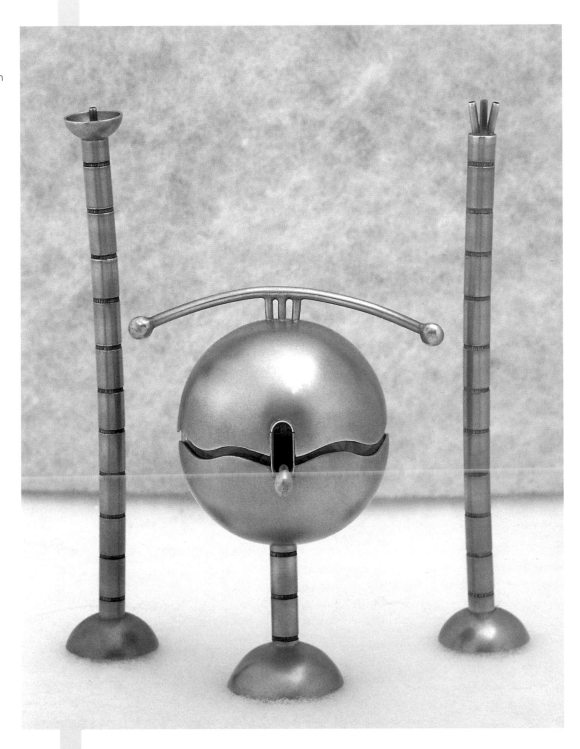

Vessel
White metal vessel with flange tipped with gilding metal.
Spun and fabricated.
28 x 30cm (11 x 11.75in)
In production

| 06.10 | Julie Chamberlain | 127 Rushmore Road |

127 Rushmore Road
Hackney
London E5 0HA
England
Tel: +44 181 533 7036

Education
MA (RCA) Silversmithing,
Royal College of Art,
London, England, 1984

Collections/commissions
Dish, The Worshipful
Company of Goldsmiths,
London, England, 1994
Collection of silverware,
AMC International,
Rotkreuz, Switzerland,
1991–95
The King George VI and
Queen Elizabeth Diamond
Stakes Trophy,
commissioned by De Beers,
London, England, 1995

06.11 **Clan Designs** **Robert McEwan**
25 Hurst View Road
South Croydon
Surrey CR2 7AJ
England
Tel: +44 181 688 1227
Fax: +44 181 681 3548

Education
BA (Hons) Silversmithing,
Sir John Cass College,
Guildhall University, London,
England, 1984
MA (RCA) Metalwork,
Royal College of Art,
London, England, 1987

Tea set
"Nessie." Sterling silver, traditional silversmithing techniques.
20 x dia. 35cm (7.75 x 13.75in)
To commission only

Tableware

"Suspended Pears." Sterling silver and stainless steel, for ripening pears in perfect condition.
45 x 45 x 45cm (17.75 x 17.75 x 17.75in)
To commission only

Tableware

"Line of Lychees." Sterling silver and stainless steel.
25 x 5 x 25 cm (9.75 x 2 x 9.75in)
To commission only

06.12	David Clarke

Unit 155
Clerkenwell Workshops
27–31 Clerkenwell Close
London EC1R 0AT
England
Tel: +44 171 490 8166
Fax: +44 171 608 3848

Education
BA (Hons) 3D Design
(Silversmithing/Metal),
Camberwell College of Art,
London, England, 1992
MA (RCA) Silversmithing,
Royal College of Art,
London, England, 1997

Collections/commissions
Royal College of Art,
permanent collection,
London, England, 1997
Production of seven pieces
for private client,
commissioned by Garrards,
London, England, 1997
Commissioned by the P&O
Makower Trust to produce
a piece for the
Victoria & Albert Museum,
London, England, 1997–98

06.13 | **Alan Pickersgill**

15 Taylor Road
Altrincham
Cheshire WA14 4LR
England
Tel: +44 161 929 0892

Education
BA (Hons) 3D Design
(Wood, Metal, Ceramics
& Glass).
Manchester Metropolitan
University, England, 1991

"I AIMED FOR A DESIGN WHICH WAS DIFFERENT FROM THE TRADITIONAL DAGGER SHAPE, YET WHICH WAS EFFECTIVE, ERGONOMIC AND SCULPTURAL."

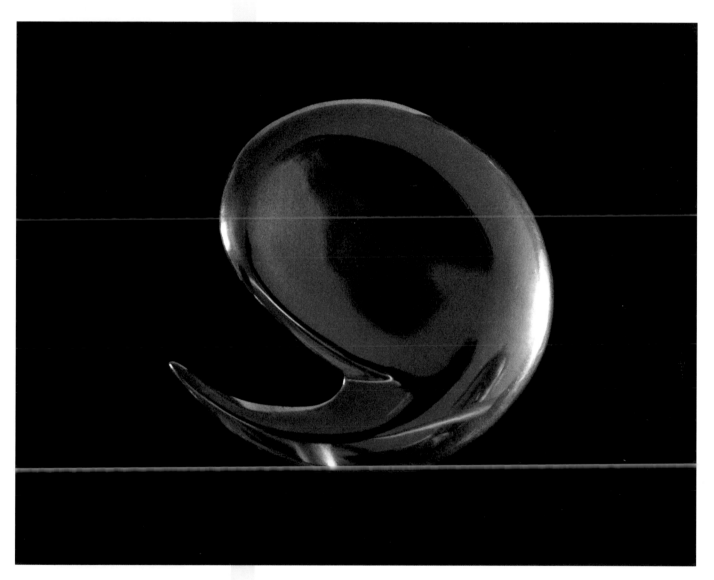

Letter knife/paperweight
Cast pewter.
Dia. 7 cm (2.75 in)
In production

06.14 **Steven Follen** Flat 1a
48 Buckingham Place
Brighton
East Sussex BN1 3PJ
England
Tel: +44 1273 327567
Fax: +44 1273 327567

Education
BA (Hons) Wood, Metal,
Ceramics & Plastics,
Brighton Polytechnic,
England, 1992

Collections/commissions
Crafts Council,
permanent collection,
London, England, 1996
South-East Arts craft
collection, Hove Museum,
England, 1993, 1997

Vessels
Coiled, welded and oxidized
steel.
62 x 8cm (24.5 x 3.25in)
To commission only

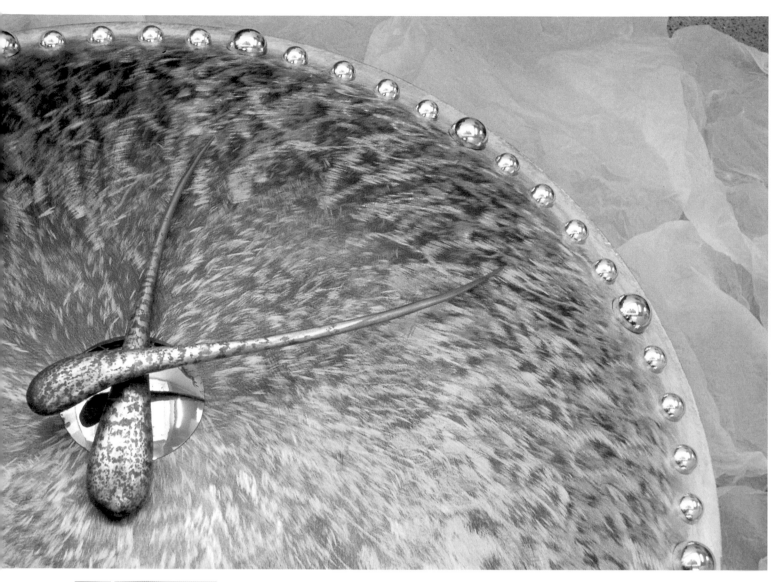

06.15   **Marianne Forrest**   Studio 4H
Leroy House
436 Essex Road
London N1 3QP
England
Tel: +44 171 359 8551
Fax: +44 171 359 8551

Education
BA (Hons) 3D Design,
Middlesex Polytechnic,
England, 1979
MA (RCA) Silversmithing,
Royal College of Art,
London, England, 1983

Collections/commissions
Pocket watch,
Royal Museum of Scotland,
Edinburgh, Scotland, 1995
Kinetic sculpture,
Royal Philharmonic Hall,
Liverpool, England, 1996
Tower clock, Spalding,
Lincolnshire, England,
1998

Clock
"Marabou." Spun aluminium, textured with a "feather" finish.
Clock hands made from beaten and treated brass.
Dia. 140cm (55in)
To commission only

06.16 | **Mila Tanya Griebel**

2 Gladys Road
West Hampstead
London NW6 2PX
England
Tel: +44 171 328 8680
Fax: +44 171 328 8680

Education
BA (Hons) 3D Design
(Metalwork),
Middlesex University,
England, 1987
MA (RCA) Silversmithing
(Metalwork & Jewellery),
Royal College of Art,
London, England, 1989

Collections/commissions
Skirball Museum,
Los Angeles, USA, 1995
The Worshipful
Company of Goldsmiths
collection, London,
England, 1996
Annual design and making of
Autocar Motor Trophies,
London, England, 1989-97

Napkin ring/egg cup
"Jester" napkin ring/egg cup.
Sterling silver, made from
sheet silver. Formed into
shape. Hand-made bobbles
applied. Hand-polished.
6 x dia. 6cm (2.45 x 2.45in)
In production

Fruit bowl
Stainless steel with mirror
finish.
43 x 43 x 20cm
(17 x 17 x 8in)
To commission only

06.17	JRH Designs

Justine Huntley
Unit 155
Clerkenwell Workshops
27-31 Clerkenwell Close
London EC1R 0AT
England
Tel: +44 171 490 8166
Fax: +44 171 608 3848

Education
BA (Hons) Silversmithing
(Metal),
Camberwell College of Art,
London, England, 1993

Collections/commissions
The Worshipful
Company of Goldsmiths
collection, London,
England, 1994
Professor Seymour
Rabinovitch, FRS,
private collection,
Washington DC, USA, 1995
Champagne breakfast tray,
Asprey, London,
England, 1997

"I AIM TO GIVE SILVER
A NEW SENSE
OF PURPOSE
FOR THE
21ST CENTURY."

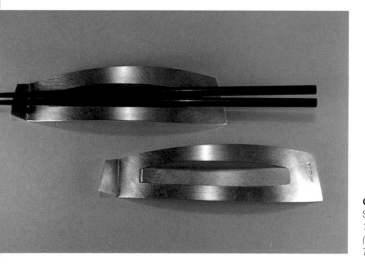

Chopstick holder
Satin finish in sterling silver.
15 x 4.25 x 2.5cm
(6 x 1.75 x 1in)
To commission only

Plate
The King George VI and
Queen Elizabeth Diamond
Stakes Trophy,
commissioned by De Beers,
London, England. Silver
chased in low relief, inlaid
with 18ct gold and set with
diamonds.
Dia. 40cm (15.75in)
To commission only

06.18 **Rod Kelly**

Providence House
East Harling
Norfolk NR16 2NQ
England
Tel: +44 1953 717625

Education
BA (Hons) Birmingham
School of Art, England, 1979
MA (RCA) Silversmithing,
Royal College of Art,
London, England, 1983

Collections/commissions
Large centrepiece (rosewater
dish and ewer), The
Worshipful Company of
Goldsmiths and The
Worshipful Company of
Fishmongers collections,
London, England, 1986
Rose bowl for the late Diana,
Princess of Wales,
commissioned by The
Worshipful Company of
Merchant Taylors, London,
England, 1990
Two large dishes and two
large silver bowls,
The Silver Trust,
10 Downing Street,
London, England, 1994

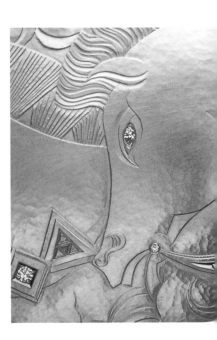

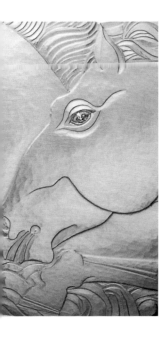

Vase
Four-sided lily vase, silver,
chased in low relief, inlaid
with fine gold.
Height 32cm (12.5in)
To commission only

"FUNCTION IS A CREATIVE GUIDELINE AND NOT A RESTRICTION UPON DESIGN."

Coffee plungers
Handmade from pewter in Sheffield, using spinning and casting techniques.
20 x dia. 10cm (8 x 4in)
In production

06.19 | Lea'd Free Designs | **Lea Denison**
Basement
Flat 2
18 St. Aubyns
Hove
East Sussex BN3 2TB
England
Tel: +44 1273 739118
Fax: +44 1273 739118

Education
BA (Hons) 3D Design,
Buckinghamshire College,
High Wycombe, England,
1994

Collections/commissions
Two trophies, BT
Environmental Supplier
Award, presented
worldwide, 1995
The Prince of Wales Trophy,
50th anniversary of
Sri Lanka's independence,
1998

Salt and pepper grinders
Sterling silver with stone detail, constructed using
silversmithing techniques, hammered surface finish.
Found pebbles indicate dark for pepper and light for salt.
16.5 x dia. 6cm (6.5 x 2.5in)
To commission only

06.20 | Cara Murphy | 22 Ballynahinch Street
Hillsborough
County Down BT26 6AW
Northern Ireland
Tel: +44 1846 689157
Fax: +44 1846 689157

Education
BA (Hons) Silversmithing &
Jewellery,
Glasgow School of Art,
Scotland, 1992
MA (RCA) Silversmithing,
Royal College of Art,
London, England, 1994

Collections/commissions
Aberdeen Art Gallery,
permanent collection,
Scotland, 1997
Shipley Art Gallery,
permanent collection,
Newcastle upon Tyne,
England, 1997
Ulster Museum,
permanent collection,
Belfast,
Northern Ireland, 1997

Tea strainer
"Starfish." Cast pewter.
3 x dia. 12cm (1.25 x 4.75in)
In production

06.21 | Nick Munro Limited | **Nick Munro**
The Canal Warehouse
Whipcord Lane
Chester
Cheshire CH1 4DE
England
Tel: +44 1244 382579
Fax: +44 1244 383712

Education
BSc Mechanical
Engineering,
Nottingham University,
England, 1984
MA (RCA) Industrial Design,
Royal College of Art,
London, England, 1986
Diploma Industrial Design,
Imperial College, London,
England, 1986

Teapot
"Cooling Tower No. 1."
Sterling silver teapot,
hand-raised and fabricated.
For use in conjunction with
gold-plated bow-leg tongs
(not illustrated).
17 x 12 x 12cm
(6.5 x 4.75 x 4.75in)
To commission only

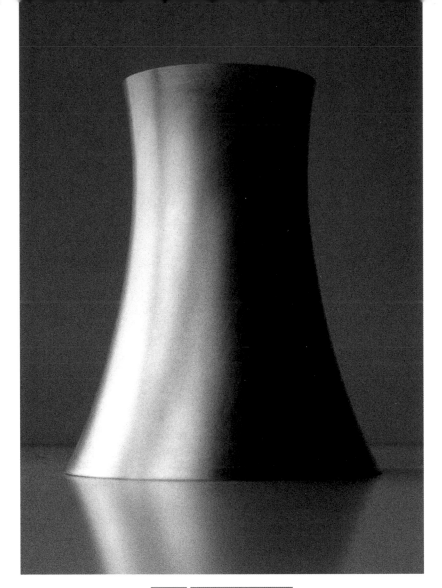

06.22	Nigel Turner Design Associates

Nigel Turner
256 Psalter Lane
Ecclesall
Sheffield
South Yorkshire S11 8UU
England
Tel: +44 114 267 9084
or +44 114 266 3084
Fax: +44 114 267 0910
E-mail: n.turner@shu.ac.uk

Education
BA (Hons) 3D Design
(Metalwork & Jewellery),
Sheffield Hallam University,
England, 1994
MA (RCA) Silversmithing
(Metalwork & Jewellery),
Royal College of Art,
London, England, 1996

Collections/commissions
Michael Petry,
private collection,
London, England, 1996
Royal College of Art,
GSMJ collection,
London, England, 1996
The Millennium Canteen,
Sheffield, England, 1997

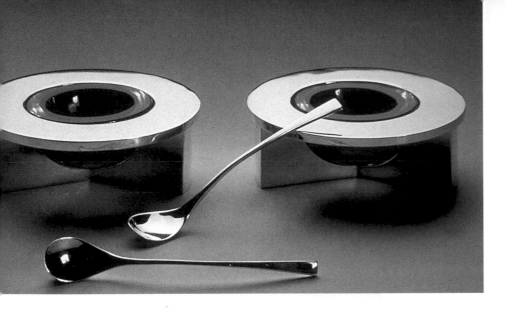

06.23 **Alfred Pain** 9 The Leathermarket
Weston Street
London SE1 3ER
England
Tel: +44 171 378 9222
Fax: +44 171 403 6381
E-mail: silver@aapi.co.uk

Education

BA (Hons) Silversmithing,
Jewellery & Allied Crafts,
London Guildhall University,
England, 1993

Collections/commissions

"Dinner for Two," Stiftung
Gold & Silberschmiedkunst,
Schwäbisch Gmünd,
Germany, 1994
Loving Cup,
Phylloxera Society,
London, England, 1997
Bowls, Living with Silver,
Asprey,
London, England, 1997

Salt cellars

Sterling silver with blown
glass interior. Spun,
handmade and assembled.
Dia. 10cm (4in)
To commission only

06.24 **Marian Power** 8 Squires Court
Binfield Road
London SW4 6TD
England
Tel: +44 171 720 5457

Education

BA (Hons) Designed
Metalwork & Jewellery,
Buckinghamshire College,
High Wycombe,
England, 1996

"I ENJOY THE CHALLENGE OF
CREATING AN OBJECT
PURELY BY CUTTING AND
FOLDING SHEET METAL."

Bowl

"Segment Bowl." Laser-cut
stainless steel sheet, formed
by curving one piece and
slotting it into the other. The
legs are then pushed
outward.
28 x 26 x 14cm
(11 x 10.25 x 5.5in)
In production

Water set
Silver and glass, gold-plated
interiors, fabricated from
sheet.
Jug 27 x 10cm
(10.75 x 4in)
Beakers 11 x 8cm
(4.25 x 3.25in)
Tray 1 x dia. 31cm
(0.5 x 12.25in)
Batch production

06.25 | **Rebecca de Quin**

Branchworks
2-4 Southgate Road
London N1 3JJ
England
Tel: +44 171 249 8878
Fax: +44 171 275 0013

Education
BA (Hons) 3D Design,
Middlesex Polytechnic,
England, 1988
MA (RCA) Metalwork &
Jewellery,
Royal College of Art,
London, England, 1990

Collections/commissions
The Worshipful
Company of Goldsmiths
collection,
London, England, 1994
Asprey,
London, England, 1997,
Crafts Council,
permanent collection,
London, England, 1998

Jugs
Silver, gold-plated handles,
fabricated from sheet.
21 x 9 x 5cm
(8.25 x 3.5 x 2in)
Prototype

Pair of water jugs
Sterling silver.
Height 40cm (15.75in)
To commission only

Interlocking candleholders
Sterling silver.
4.5 x 15 x 4.5cm (1.75 x 6 x 1.75in)
In production

**Justin Richardson and
Steve Ottewill**
Evegate
Station Road
Smeeth
Ashford
Kent TN25 6SX
England
Tel: +44 1303 814484
Fax: +44 1303 814730

Education
Justin Richardson - BTEC
HND, Silversmithing,
Kent Institute of Art &
Design, England, 1990
Steve Ottewill - BTEC HND,
Silversmithing,
Kent Institute of Art & Design,
England, 1989

Collections/commissions
Professor Seymour
Rabinovitch, FRS,
private collection,
Washington DC, USA, 1994
Chalice and paten,
Canterbury Cathedral,
England, 1995
Endeavour Trophy for the
Intelligence Corps,
The Worshipful Company
of Painters & Stainers,
London, England, 1996

Coffee pot
Sterling silver.
Height 28cm (11in)
To commission only

07 Interior Accessories

Introduction
Peta Levi

This chapter on interior accessories depicts a wide variety of products, from CD racks to a laundry bin and a sushi setting. On the one hand, there are many young designers applying their craft skills to make accessories or beautiful items for the home. For instance, a growing number of woodturners are making treen, wooden objects which acquire even greater beauty with age. Others are making a tremendous variety of interesting mirrors, of which we are showing two.

One mirror, by Rebecca Newnham (see page 202), is made of mosaics, the material in which she works, whether to create fountains and bar tops or murals for private bathrooms or ocean liners. Her simpler mosaic mirrors can be bought in retail stores, or you can commission more elaborate pieces. The other mirror shown is by Caroline Le Cras (see page 199), who uses old techniques, including *verre eglomisé*, gesso, silvering and gilding. In the UK these techniques are only taught by the City & Guilds of London Art School, and Caroline is one of a growing group of graduates who apply these techniques in a contemporary manner, mostly to decorate mirrors and furniture.

On the other hand, other designers, in particular furniture designers, are now applying their minds to design accessories for the purely

Vase by Inflate
"Star" vase. Vacuum-formed
PVC, welded to flexible PVC.
35 x 35 x 14cm
(13.75 x 13.75 x 5.5in)
In production

Fruit bowl by Inflate
HF-welded, inflatable PVC
structure.
38 x 38 x 27cm
(15 x 15 x 10.5in)
In production

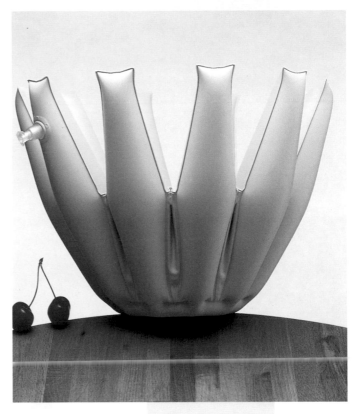

practical reason that it is easier to sell accessories than furniture.
Accessories tend to be mass-produced, and they often create a
much-needed regular income, giving the designer the time that is
usually needed to market furniture successfully.

I see it as a healthy and exciting step forward when a jeweller, Lin
Cheung, designs a useful picnic tool which can be kept in one's
pocket and brought out to eat lunch (see page 194), and when
designers such as the Inflate team and Sebastian Bergne start
designing everyday objects such as kitchen storage jars and a
soap ring, peg and brushes (see page 192). In a similar vein, Mark
Gabbertas has designed smart coat hangers, turning what can be
a dull and unsightly item into a sculptural form when not in use
(see page 197).

At first glance this chapter may appear to show a strange
assortment of artefacts - a ring tree, turned wood, table mats
and an egg rack, for example. However, the potential for these
designers to create innovative objects for everyday use is enormous.
I believe that designers will increasingly use their ingenuity to make
accessories for the home and the office that will be both more
stylish and also more fun to use than the more mundane items that
are currently available.

"I BELIEVE THAT DESIGNERS WILL INCREASINGLY USE THEIR
INGENUITY TO MAKE ACCESSORIES
FOR THE HOME AND THE OFFICE THAT WILL BE BOTH
MORE STYLISH AND ALSO MORE FUN
TO USE THAN WHAT IS CURRENTLY AVAILABLE."

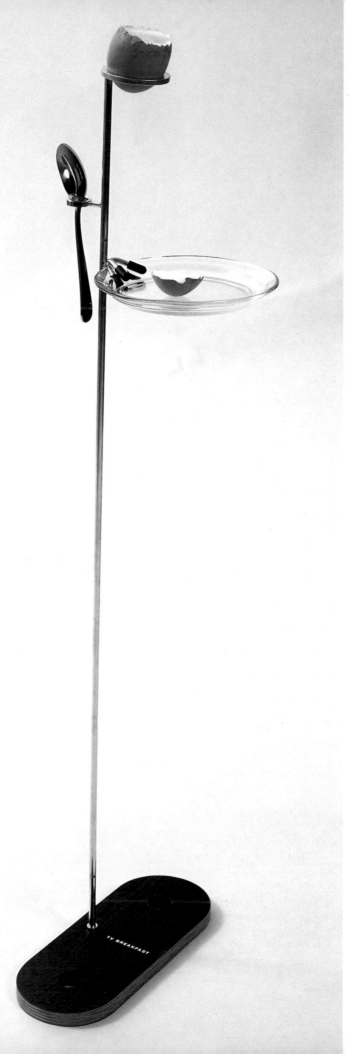

07.01   **Pascal Anson**   48 Rennie Court
Upper Ground
London SE1 9LP
England
Tel: +44 171 620 0261
Fax: +44 171 620 0261

Education
BA (Hons) Furniture &
Product Design,
Kingston University,
England, 1995

Egg cup
"TV Breakfast". Chrome-
plated mild steel, Pyrex
plate, ply and laminate base.
Height 72cm (28.5in)
In production

Drinks mat/coaster
"Bubblo-mat". Injected
moulded plastic.
0.75cm x dia. 8.75
(0.25 x 3.5in)
In production

07.02	Angels (Mouldings)

Jonathan Boston
72a Abbeydale Road
Sheffield
South Yorkshire S7 1FD
England
Tel: +44 114 255 2952
Fax: +44 114 255 3004
E-mail: info@bubblo-mat.com
Website: www.bubblo-mat.com

Salt and pepper pots
"Moo Cows". Injection-
moulded plastic salt and
pepper set that contains a
mechanical noise box that
"moos" when turned upside-
down.
9.5 x 8 x 11cm
(3.75 x 3 x 4.5in)
In production

07.03	Philip Watts Design

Philip Watts
32b Shakespeare Street
Nottingham NG1 4FQ
England
Tel: +44 1159 474809
Fax: +44 1159 475828

Education
BA (Hons) Furniture &
Product Design,
Nottingham Trent University,
England, 1992

Collections/commissions
Shimla Pinks, restaurant
interiors in Glasgow,
Scotland, and Birmingham,
Nottingham and Oxfordshire,
England, 1997-98
Reception interior,
McCarthy Corporation,
Kensington, London,
England, 1997
Ronen Chen, ladies fashion
retail interior, London,
England, 1997

Sebastian Bergne
2 Ingate Place
London SW8 3NS
England
Tel: +44 171 622 3333
Fax: +44 171 622 3336

Education
BA (Hons) Industrial Design
(Engineering),
Central St Martins College
of Art & Design,
London, England, 1988
MDes (RCA) Industrial
Design, Royal College of Art,
London, England, 1990

Collections/commissions
Lampshade,
Design Museum,
permanent collection,
London, England, 1996
Lampshade and "Spira"
flexible ballpoint pen,
mutant materials collection,
Museum of Modern Art,
New York, USA, 1996

Pepper mill
"Funnel top" pepper mill by Shin Azumi. This pepper mill
borrows its name from the shape of its grinder. The funnel
top, which provides a good grip, also facilitates the refilling of
the mill. Beech, American walnut, pepper mill mechanism.
11 x dia. 7cm (4.5 x 2.75in)
In production

Shin and Tomoko Azumi
Ground Floor
953 Finchley Road
London NW11 7PE
England
Tel: +44 181 731 7496
Fax: +44 181 731 7496

Education
Shin Azumi - BA (Hons)
Product Design,
Kyoto City University of Art,
Japan, 1989
MA (RCA) Industrial Design,
Royal College of Art,
London, England, 1994
Tomoko Azumi - BA (Hons)
Environmental Design,
Kyoto City University of Art,
Japan, 1989
MA (RCA) Furniture Design,
Royal College of Art,
London, England, 1995

Collections/commissions
Crafts Council,
permanent collection,
London, England, 1995
Geffrye Design Museum
collection, London, England,
1996
Victoria & Albert Museum,
permanent collection,
London, England, 1997

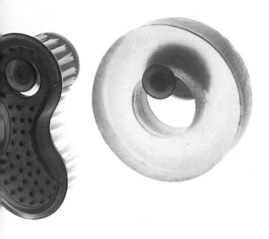

Soap ring, peg and brushes
A ring of natural glycerine soap that is stored by hanging on a plastic peg. The soap always remains dry and in turn becomes a graphic element in the bathroom or kitchen. The product family has since been extended with injection-moulded washing-up and scrubbing brushes.
Manufactured by Authentics, Germany.
Soap ring 2 x dia. 7.5cm (0.75 x 3in)
Scrubbing brush 4 x 9 x 4.5 (1.5 x 3.5 x 1.75in)
Washing-up brush 4.5 x 21 x 4.5cm (1.75 x 8.25 x 1.75in)
In production

07.06	Arkitype Design Partnership	Douglas Bryden, Richard Smith and Stephen Young

1 Somerset Place
Charing Cross
Glasgow G3 7JT
Scotland
Tel: +44 141 333 1132
Fax: +44 141 333 1132

Education
Douglas Bryden, Richard Smith and Stephen Young — all BA (Hons) Product Design, Glasgow School of Art, Scotland, 1996

Collections/commissions
National Trust of Scotland for The Hill House, Helensburgh, Scotland, 1998

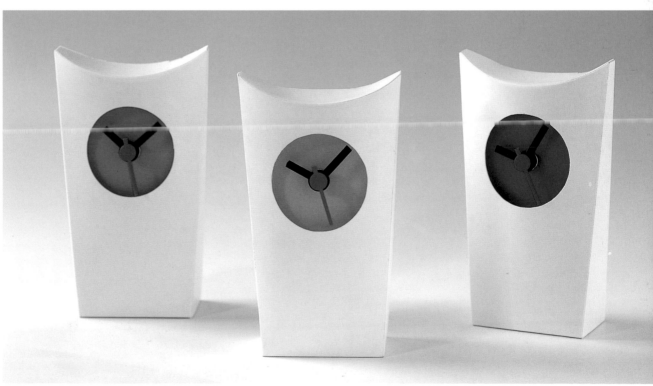

Clock
"Solo" clock. Cold-stamped polypropylene plastic. Flat-pack assembly.
16.5 x 9.5 x 3.75cm (6.5 x 3.75 x 1.5in)
In production

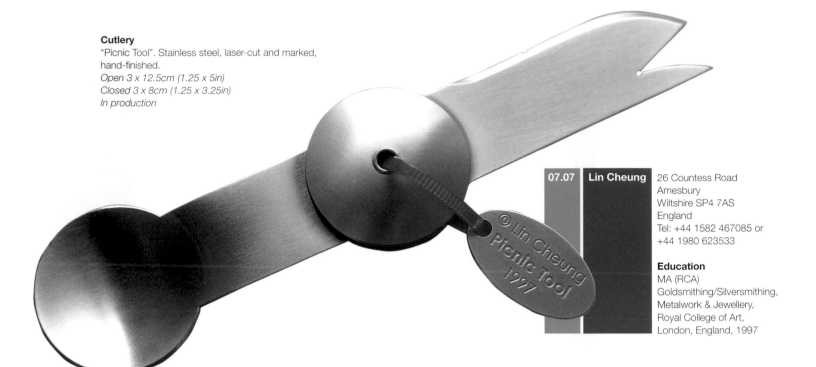

Cutlery
"Picnic Tool". Stainless steel, laser-cut and marked, hand-finished.
Open 3 x 12.5cm (1.25 x 5in)
Closed 3 x 8cm (1.25 x 3.25in)
In production

| 07.07 | **Lin Cheung** | 26 Countess Road
Amesbury
Wiltshire SP4 7AS
England
Tel: +44 1582 467085 or
+44 1980 623533 |

Education
MA (RCA)
Goldsmithing/Silversmithing,
Metalwork & Jewellery,
Royal College of Art,
London, England, 1997

Tray
"Artichoke". Photographic image produced by scanning a high-resolution photograph and producing four-colour chromalin film to print the foils to set in the melamine tray.
50 x 38cm (19.5 x 15in)
In production

| 07.08 | **Ella Doran** | 1 Tenter Ground
London E1 7NH
England
Tel: +44 171 375 1466
Fax: +44 171 375 0366
Website: www.i-i.net/elladoran/

Education
BA (Hons) Printed Textiles,
Middlesex University,
England, 1993

Collections/commissions
Exclusive range of table mats based on botanicals and architecture,
Kew Gardens,
London, England, 1997
Exclusive range of table mats, Heal's,
London, England, 1997
Photographs taken for a new graphic look at the library archives, Bodleian Library,
Oxford, England, 1997

**Pat Booth and
Nina Moeller**
Steam Museum
Green Dragon Lane
Brentford
Middlesex TW8 0EN
England
Tel: +44 171 602 9344
or +44 1932 827447
Fax: +44 171 602 9344
or +44 1932 827447

Education
Pat Booth —
Mixed Media, Banff Centre,
Alberta, Canada, 1982
Cabinet Making,
London College of Furniture,
England, 1989
Workshop,
Hooke Park College,
Dorset, England, 1991
Nina Moeller —
Apprenticeship in
cabinetmaking in small firm
in Bremerhaven,
Germany, 1984–87
Designing and Making in
Wood,
Parnham College,
Dorset, England, 1989

Collections/commissions
Oak and leather upholstered
stacking chairs and bar
tables, private function room,
Ivy Restaurant,
London, England, 1994
Large reception desk,
Independent Living Centre,
Essex County Council,
Bishops Stortford,
Essex, England, 1996
Boardroom table for British
Consulate General,
Düsseldorf, Germany, 1997

Shelf
"Quadrant" shelf. Wall-mounted unit, laminated birch ply with
mirror front and glass shelves.
46 x 46 x 110cm (18 x 18 x 43.5in)
In production

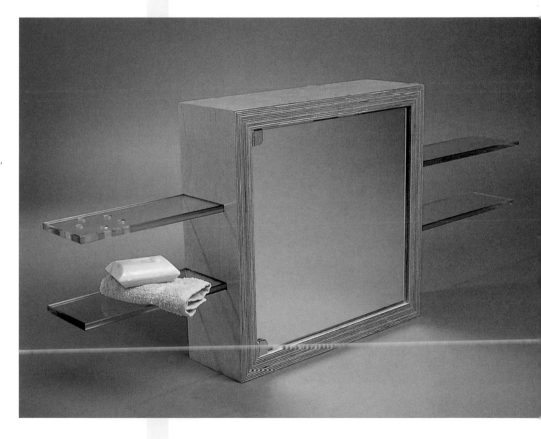

Shelving
"Scoop" ceramic shelving. Slip-cast white earthenware, glazed.
8 x 16 x 9cm (3 x 6.25 x 3.5in)
In production

"MY PURPOSE IS TO
TO FIND NEW POTENTIAL
IN TRADITIONAL FORMS,
DECONSTRUCTING
AND JUXTAPOSING
COMPONENTS TO CREATE
DYNAMIC, FUNCTIONAL
COMPOSITIONS."

| 07.10 | In Situ | **Julia Pitts** |

Number Six
Whiston
Northampton NN7 1NN
England
Tel: +44 1604 890536
Fax: +44 1604 810413

Education
BA (Hons) Interior Design,
Nottingham Trent University,
England, 1991
Postgraduate Diploma
Ceramics,
Goldsmiths College,
London, England, 1993

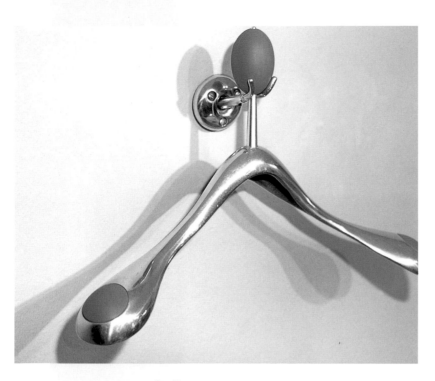

Coathanger
"The Headhanger". Die-cast polished aluminium body with silicon rubber head and shoulders, ceiling or wall-mounted bracket systems.
30 x 45 x 12cm (12 x 17.5 x 4.5in)
In production

07.11 | Gabbertas | **Mark Gabbertas**
Oblique Workshops
Stamford Works
Gillett Street
London N16 8JH
England
Tel: +44 171 503 2112
Fax: +44 171 275 7495
E-mail:
gabbers@gabbertas.demon.co.uk

Education
BA (Hons) Political Philosophy and Geography, Durham University, England, 1983

Collections/commissions
Atelier restaurant, London, England, 1996
Allermuir, "30" range of chairs/tables and "Tubby" range of chairs/tables, Darwen, England, 1997
Head Office, M & C Saatchi, London, England, 1997

07.12 | **JAM Design & Communications** | **Jamie Anley, Astrid Zala and Matthieu Paillard**
Top Floor, 1 Goodsway
Kings Cross
London NW1 1UR
England
Tel: +44 171 278 5567
Fax: +44 171 278 3263

Education
Jamie Anley —
BSc Architecture, Bartlett School of Architecture, University College of London, England, 1995
Astrid Zala —
BA (Hons) Fine Art, Goldsmiths College, London, England, 1991
Matthieu Paillard -
Architectural Apprentice, Valfort Design, Nice, France, 1993

Collections/commissions
Manchester City Arts Council, permanent collection, England, 1997
Norman bar/restaurant, Leeds, England, 1997
Guggenheim Museum, SoHo, New York, USA, 1998

Vase
"Buoy". In conjunction with Zotefoams, JAM have developed a range of accessories and furniture exploring new ways of using a hi-tech foam material within a new design context. Each piece is machined using CNC routing technology.
12 x dia. 24.5cm (4.5 x 9.5in)
In production

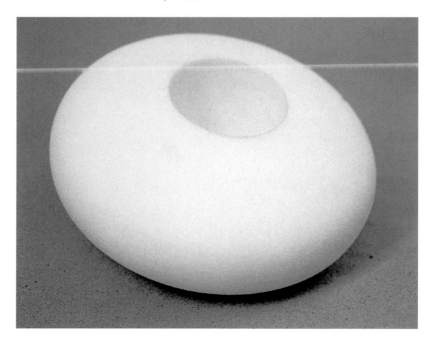

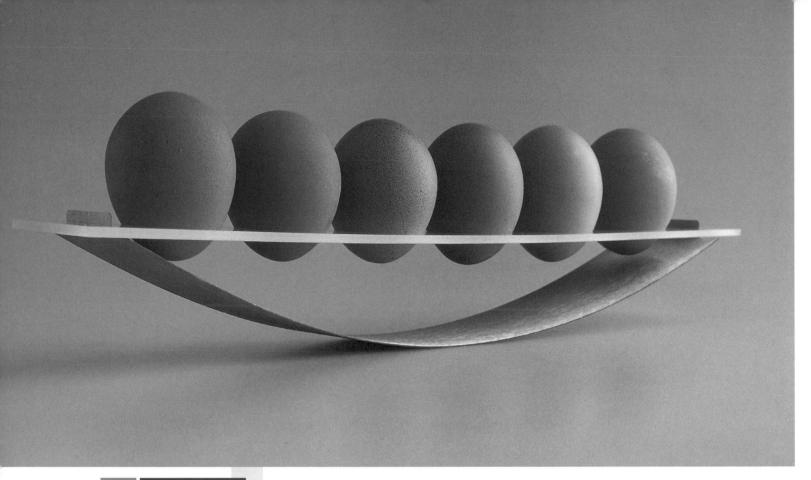

| 07.13 | Lea'd Free Designs | **Lea Denison**
Basement, Flat 2
18 St. Aubyns
Hove
East Sussex BN3 2TB
England
Tel: +44 1273 739118
Fax: +44 1273 739118

Education
BA (Hons) 3D Design,
Buckinghamshire College,
High Wycombe, England,
1994

Collections/commissions
Two trophies,
BT Environmental Supplier
Award,
presented worldwide, 1995
The Prince of Wales Trophy,
50th anniversary of
Sri Lanka's independence,
1998

Egg rack
"Egg Racking System". Flat-pack, stainless steel and perspex.
5 x 5 x 34cm (2 x 2 x 13.5in)
In production

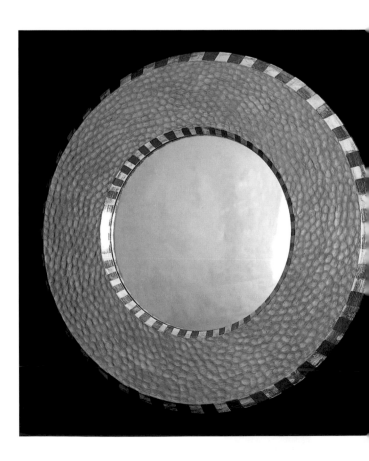

Gilded mirror with silver-leaf glass
"Round Mirror". Frame-gilded using traditional techniques -
gesso and bole, with a distressed gold-leaf finish. Mirror of
convex glass, gilded with silver leaf.
Dia. 68cm (26.75in)
To commission only

07.14 **Keith Lobban**

The Studios
Potato Town
Great Tew
Chipping Norton
Oxfordshire OX7 4AP
England
Tel: +44 1608 683323
Fax: +44 1608 683323

Education
Designing and Making in
Wood, Parnham College,
Dorset, England, 1994

Collections/commissions
Ten dining chairs in steam-
bent oak, private
commission, Bad Driburg,
Germany, 1996
Two hall stands, slate and
oak, private commission,
Dublin, Ireland, 1996
Dining table and twelve
chairs in solid oak, private
commission, Surrey,
England, 1998

07.15 **Caroline Le Cras**

Brewhurst
Brewhurst Lane
Loxwood
West Sussex RH14 0RJ
England
Tel: +44 1403 753710
Fax: +44 1403 752353

Education
Diploma Decorative Arts,
City & Guilds London Art
School
London, England, 1988

Collections/commissions
Private collections
worldwide

CD rack
Compact disks are stored on sliding shelves which hold a
maximum of 120 CDs. Made from sycamore and
stainless steel.
102 x 26 x 14cm (40 x 10.25 x 5.5in)
To commission only

07.16 **Maké Design Limited**

Li Marhaban
Unit 8
1 Fawe Street
London E14 6PD
England
Tel: +44 171 377 0858
Fax: +44 171 377 0858

Education
BA (Hons) 3D Design,
Polytechnic Southwest,
Exeter, England, 1991
Furniture Woodcraft,
London Guildhall University,
England, 1994

Collections/commissions
Museum of Modern Art, New
York, USA, 1997
Mr Jack Lansbury OBE
(Royal Opera House
conductor),
London, England, 1997

Magazine rack
"UBI". Made from single pieces of layered birch aeroply using
one-piece moulding technique.
34.5 x 21 x 37.5cm (13.5 x 8.25 x 14.75in)
In production

Vase, ring tree and pot
Turned rosewood and slip-cast ceramic.
Vase 20.5 x dia. 6.5cm (8 x 2.5in)
Ring tree 18.5 x dia. 6cm (7.25 x 2.5in)
Pot 8 x dia. 7cm (3.25 x 2.75in)
In production

07.17 **Michael Sodeau Partnership**

**Michael Sodeau
and Lisa Giuliani**
24 Rosebery Avenue
London EC1R 4SX
England
Tel: +44 171 837 2343
Fax: +44 171 837 2343

Education
Michael Sodeau —
BA (Hons) Product Design,
Central St Martins College
of Art & Design,
London, England, 1994

Platter
"Stripes". Hand-made black, white and green glass platter,
fused and slumped, with dichroic detail.
30 x 30cm (12 x 12in)
To commission only

07.18	Mosquito

Amy Cushing
62 Lower Ham Road
Kingston upon Thames
Surrey KT2 5AW
England
Tel: +44 181 715 5611
Fax: +44 181 949 4490

Education
BA (Hons) Mural Design,
Chelsea School of Art,
London, England, 1992

Collections/commissions
Glass platters presented at
Premier Childrenswear
Fashion Award,
Birmingham, England, 1996
Custom-made ceramic and
glass tiles for select bars in
London, Newcastle upon
Tyne and Leeds, England,
1998

07.19 Rebecca Newnham

Palmerston
Kingston
Ringwood
Hampshire BH24 3BG
England
Tel: +44 1425 474736
Fax: +44 1425 474736

Education

BA (Hons) Design,
Staffordshire University,
England, 1988
MA (RCA) Ceramics & Glass,
Royal College of Art,
London, England, 1991

Collections/commissions

Wall mural for Accident &
Emergency Department,
Forrest Heath Care,
Whipps Cross Hospital,
London, England, 1993
Two "Mayan Serpents",
mosaic sculptures,
Royal Caribbean
International, Miami,
USA, 1997
"Tree of Life and
Knowledge", mosaic
sculpture,
Royal Caribbean
International, Miami,
USA, 1997

Mirror
"Zen". Mirrored mosaic with MDF back.
Dia. 100cm (39.5in)
In production

Vessel
French oak base, ash vessel.
Vessel coloured ultramarine
blue acrylic, braided around
with monofilament and
sandblasted. Blue resin in
base and vessel.
122 x 43cm (48 x 17in)
To commission only

07.20 Victoria Overton

Kizzie Cottage
81 Bell Common
Epping
Essex CM16 4DZ
England
Tel: +44 1992 560428
Fax: +44 1992 560428

Education

BA (Hons) Craft,
Manchester Metropolitan
University, England, 1997

Zen platform with bowl
Polished ceramic bowl available in a number of finishes.
Platform of acid-etched concrete, also available in a number
of finishes.
Bowl 15 x dia. 51cm (6 x 20in)
Platform 4 x 75 x 170cm (1.5 x 29.5 x 67in)
To commission only

07.21 **Julie Wood** 87 Waldegrave Road
Brighton
East Sussex BN1 6GJ
England
Tel: +44 1273 702998
Fax: +44 1273 702998

Education
BA (Hons) 3D Design,
Brighton Polytechnic,
England, 1989
MA (RCA) Ceramics & Glass,
Royal College of Art,
London, England, 1991

Collections/commissions
Contemporary Art Society,
London, England, 1993
Walker Art Gallery collection,
Liverpool, England, 1996
York City Art Gallery
Collection, England, 1996

CD and tape rack
"Interlok". Available in three modular kit shapes for storage
system of any shape or size, allowing easy organisation of
large music collections. Model shown, "Square" kit, to hold
120 CDs/112 tapes.
72 x 81 x 6.5cm (28.25 x 32 x 2.5in)
In production

07.22 **Artefice Design** **Peter Forbes**
13 Macklin House
Shackleton Close
London SE23 3YP
England
Tel: +44 181 699 2756
Fax: +44 181 699 2756
E-mail: artefice@mcmail.com

Education
BSc (Hons) Electrical
Engineering,
UMIST,
Manchester, England, 1986
BSc (Hons) Engineering
Product Design,
South Bank University,
London, England, 1995

Collections/commissions
Electronics for interactive
audio-visual consoles, in
conjunction with Diane
Harris, "Hex" and "Coldcut",
The Bomb nightclub,
Nottingham, England, 1997
Interactive audio-visual
installation,
The London Aquarium,
County Hall,
London, England, 1998

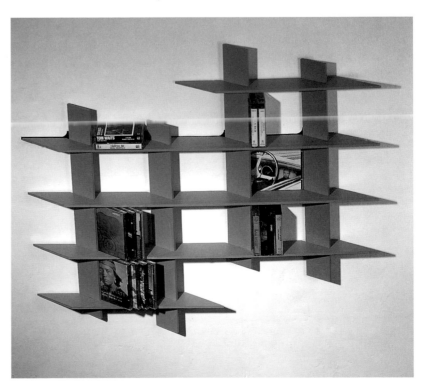

07.23 **Sam Design Limited**

Simon Maidment
Basement
108 Huddleston Road
Islington
London N7 0EG
England
Tel: +44 171 272 8294
Fax: +44 171 272 8294

Education
MA (RCA) Furniture,
Royal College of Art,
London, England, 1992

Collections/commissions
"Baby Tambour" chair,
Vitra Design Museum,
permanent collection,
Weil am Rhein, Germany,
1998

Candlestick
"Bloop". Cast polyurethane
resin, aluminium spinning.
18 x dia. 12cm
(7 x 4.75in)
In production

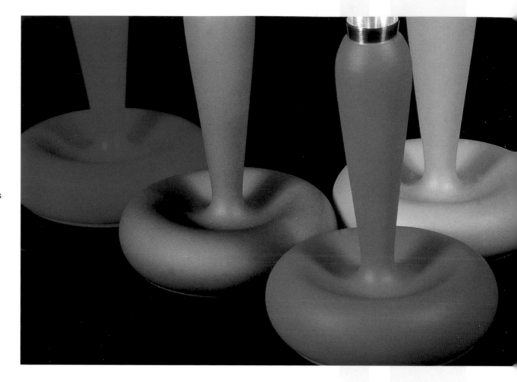

Magazine rack
"Match". Made from
3mm sheet steel, painted.
43 x 28 x 28cm
(17 x 11 x 11in)
In production

"DESIGN IS NOT
THE SAUCE ADDED
TO A DISH,
IT IS THE
COOKING ITSELF."

07.24 **Winfried Scheuer**
52 Leinster Square
London W2 4PU
England
Tel: +44 171 221 1020
Fax: +44 171 221 2765
E-mail:
winfried@dezign.demon.co.uk

Education
MA (RCA) Industrial Design,
Royal College of Art,
London, England, 1981

07.25 | **Mary Ann Simmons**

69 Wellington Row
London E2 7BB
England
Tel: +44 171 739 1763
Fax: +44 171 739 1763
E-mail: silver@aapi.co.uk

Education
BA (Hons) Silversmithing, Jewellery & Applied Crafts, London Guildhall University, England, 1997

Sushi place setting
Sterling silver and elm wood. Main plate scored and folded, two spun dishes, sake/tea cup hand-raised.
Elm wood block 4 x 25 x 48cm (1.5 x 10 x 19in)
Silver plate 25 x 13cm (10 x 5in)
Silver dishes dia. 9.5cm (3.75in)
Sake/tea cup dia. 4.5cm (1.75in)
To commission only

Laundry box
"Joey". Laundry box with three curved sides and hinged lid. Maple and birch ply.
42 x 50 x 74cm
(17 x 20 x 29.5in)
In production

07.26 | **Stemmer & Sharp**

Andrea Stemmer
2 Wren Street
London WC1X 0HA
England
Tel: +44 171 503 2105
Fax: +44 171 275 7495

Education
Designing and Making in Wood, Parnham College, Dorset, England, 1989

Collections/commissions
Furniture for three executive offices, Clinic Catering Services, Düsseldorf, Germany, 1995
Refurbishment of entrance hall, comprising reception desk, sales counter, sales area, shelving and storage cabinets, postcard racks and notice boards, Hove Museum & Art Gallery, England, 1996
Garden furniture comprising four chairs, two benches and three tables, M and Mme Malouf, Antibes, France, 1997

07.27 | **Pete Stevens** | 35 Water Lane
Melbourn
Cambridgeshire SG8 6AY
England
Tel: +44 1763 261858
Website:
www.candidarts.com

Education
BA (Hons) Visual Arts,
Camberwell College of Art,
London, England, 1997

Chopsticks and bowls
Thrown stoneware bowls with applied palladium leaf, and
forged silver chopsticks.
Large bowl dia. 21cm (8.25in)
To commission only

Bottle opener
"Void" bottle opener. Electropolished stainless steel tube.
Dia. 1.8 x 16cm (0.75 x 6.5in)
In production

07.28 | **Stephen Philips** | 52 Park Street
Thame
Oxfordshire OX9 3HS
England
Tel: +44 1844 214897
Fax: +44 1844 214897

Education
BA (Hons) Furniture &
Product Design,
Buckinghamshire College,
High Wycombe, England,
1992

Collections/commissions
Seating commissioned by
Hampshire Architects
School, Eastleigh, England,
1994
Interactive reception area for
In Real Life, design
competition winner,
London, England, 1996

Wine rack
Flexible transparent PVC,
supports ten bottles. Each
PVC unit is die-stamped and
suspended from a bright
nickel-plated mild steel split
ring, hook and pair of
washers.
Runner-up, Blueprint Design
Awards 1997.
150 x 30cm (59 x 12in)
In production

07.29 | **Jo Tracey**

51 Newtown
Hullavington
Wiltshire SN14 6EQ
England
Tel: +44 1666 837531
Fax: +44 1666 837531

Education
BA (Hons) 3D Design
(Furniture), Leeds
Metropolitan University,
England, 1996

Collections/commissions
David Ryb, Mercutio Design,
London, England, 1998

08Furniture

Introduction
Michael Marriott

In the Introduction I explained how the revival in the 1990s of interest in furniture design had a direct link with the Arts and Crafts Movement at the turn of the 20th century. By the 1980s Ann Hartree had become a catalyst in making people aware of the new furniture designer/makers. With the help of Anne Crossman, the widow of British Labour politician Richard Crossman, Hartree started Prescote, a pioneering gallery for contemporary craft — and in particular furniture. People from all over the world visited the gallery, which was housed in converted stables in the Oxfordshire countryside, near Banbury. It was thus that the public became aware of the remarkable revival of the making of individual pieces of contemporary furniture.

The New Designers exhibitions, the first of which took place in 1985, triggered a more commercial approach from design graduates, who began to think about having their products batch-produced and mass-produced. Since then, of course, young British designers have experienced many problems, both in getting their products manufactured and in marketing them successfully. However, a lead was taken by several London-based shops which operate as retailers and wholesalers. In 1986 Sheridan Coackley started SCP, which has helped some of Britain's most important furniture designers — including Jasper Morrison, Matthew Hilton and Terence Woodgate — to develop their designs by manufacturing, wholesaling and retailing the products. International recognition of these designers helped to establish the UK as an interesting and important source of contemporary design. James Maier established Viaduct in 1989, and that company has also played its part in getting British

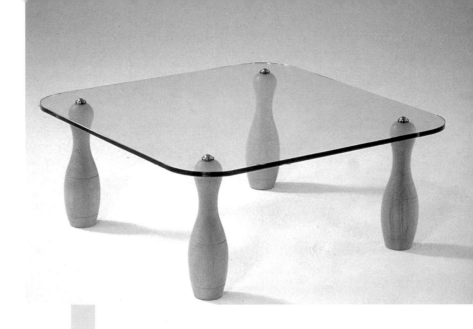

Coffee Table
"Skittle". Designed by
Michael Marriott for SCP
Limited. Turned beech legs,
toughened glass top.
*75 x 75 x 32cm
(29.5 x 29.5 x 12.5in)
In production*
SCP Limited
135 139 Curtain Road
London EC1A 3BX
England

designs manufactured. In 1991 Paul Newman started Aero, a shop in Bayswater in West London, which sells contemporary furniture and accessories and has helped some 15 designers to manufacture and market their designs.

A handful of British manufacturers are now picking up on this design talent. Ness Furniture Limited is manufacturing a lounge chair by Nick Delo (see page 253) and a café chair by Robert Kilvington; Allermuir Contract Furniture Ltd. manufactures pieces by, among other British designers, Amos Marchant (see page 235); Aram Design has developed a range of contract seating by Rock Galpin (see page 256), and Englender Limited works with a number of British designers, including Richard Woolf of McDaniel Woolf, who designed a collection of tables for the Japanese retailer Muji (see pages 236/7).

However, most designers have to struggle on their own. Nevertheless, some of them are exploring new materials and technologies and trying to source reliable subcontractors. Jane Atfield has even started her own company, Made of Waste, which recycles plastic to make a sheet material which she exports to, among other countries, Germany, France and Japan. She also designs and makes furniture and accessories from this material (see page 228).

I think that the future is bright for Britain's furniture designers.

Peta Levi MBE

Recent years have seen a major increase in "Do-It-Yourself" – commonly abbreviated to DIY – as a leisure activity in Britain. One illustration of this is the growing number and size of out-of-town superstores. I recently visited the largest branch of B&Q, just outside Glasgow, in Scotland, where you can almost see the curvature of the earth between the aisles.

The same period has also seen the demise of a large part of Britain's manufacturing industry – a development responsible for the increase in another kind of DIY. Every year another batch of furniture and product graduates are dispatched into a world where they are often obliged to do it themselves.

DIY manufacturing puts the designers in a position where they are forced to tackle things in a hands-on way. This provokes a more thorough understanding of materials, processes and their applications, therefore providing an excellent real world training for the development and production of ideas.

The resultant culture is lively, fresh and eclectic. It illustrates the many niches where design can survive despite global branding and marketing. Ironically it is also allowing a new, vibrant and ultimately flexible counter-industry to evolve. Many of the products of that counter-industry are described in this book.

Michael Marriott

THE RESULTANT CULTURE IS LIVELY, FRESH AND ECLECTIC. IT ILLUSTRATES THE MANY NICHES WHERE DESIGN CAN SURVIVE DESPITE GLOBAL BRANDING AND MARKETING.

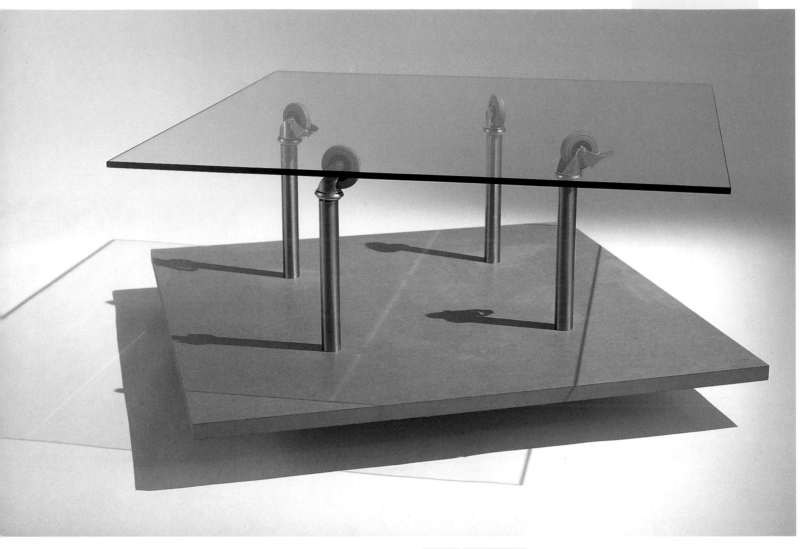

Table
Adjustable table from the turning tables series. Glass, steel,
castors and MDF. Glass surface rolls on castors and can be
fixed in any position by applying castor brakes.
40 x 90 x 90cm (15.75 x 35.5 x 35.5in)
Prototype

08.01 **Ralph Ball** 177 Waller Road
London SE14 5LX
England
Tel: + 44 171 635 8792
or + 44 171 590 4323
Fax:+ 44 171 635 8792
or + 44 171 590 4320

Education
MA (RCA) Furniture Design,
Royal College of Art,
London, England, 1980

Collections/commissions
Museum of Modern Art,
permanent collection,
New York , USA, 1987
Crafts Council,
permanent collection,
London, England, 1984

08.02 **Aero** **Nazanin Kamali**
96 Westbourne Grove
London W2 5RT
England
Tel:+44 171 221 1950
Fax:+44 171 221 2555
E-mail:
info@aero-furniture.com
Website:
www.aero-furniture.com

Education
MA (RCA) Furniture Design,
Royal College of Art,
London, England, 1991

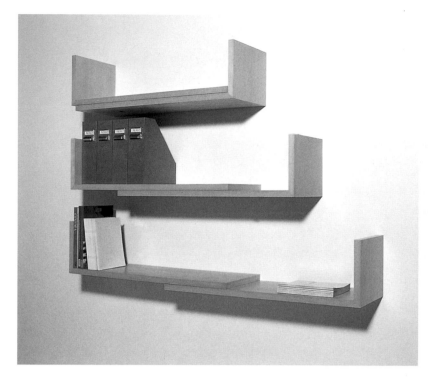

Shelf
Extending shelf, beech
veneered MDF.
*25 x 30 x 93–142cm
(10 x 12 x 36.5–56in)
Prototype*

Stools
"The Link". Bent tubular
steel frame with moulded
plywood seat.
Runner-up in the public
seating competition for the
Natural History Museum,
London, England, 1007
*45 x 52 x 36cm
(17.75 x 20.5 x 14in)
Prototype*

08.03 **Chris Bailey** c/o A. D Creative
Consultants Limited
The Royal Victoria Patriotic
Building
Trinity Road
London SW18 3SX
England
Tel:+44 181 870 8743
Fax:+44 181 877 1151
E-mail:cbailey889@aol.com

Education
BA (Hons) Furniture &
Related Products,
Buckinghamshire College,
High Wycombe, England,
1997

08.04 | **Bius** | **Mary Little**
37 Henty Close
London SW11 4AH
England
Tel: +44 171 585 1100
Fax: +44 171 924 6524
E-mail: bius@globalnet.co.uk

Education
BA (Hons) Furniture Design,
Ulster Polytechnic, Belfast,
Northern Ireland, 1981
MDes (RCA) Furniture
Design, Royal College of Art,
London, England, 1985

Collections/commissions
Musée des Arts Decoratifs,
Paris, France, 1987
Victoria & Albert Museum,
London, England, 1994
Ulster Museum, Belfast,
Northern Ireland, 1996

Chair
"Airchair". White glass fibre seat, satin-polished stainless steel
frame and white nylon turned feet. Components made in
various small factories.
69 x 78 x dia. 50cm (27 x 30.5 x 19.5in)
To commission only

08.05 | **Ou Baholyodhin** | Unit 18
1b Darnley Road
London E9 6QH
England
Tel: +44 181 525 5353
Fax: +44 181 525 5354

Education
BSc (Hons) International
Relations, London School of
Economics, England, 1989
BA (Hons) Furniture &
Product Design,
Kingston University,
England, 1996

Chair
"HK97" chair in stainless steel. Made to commemorate the
handover of Hong Kong. Classic architectural form derived
from Ming dynasty scholar's chair, "Wen Yi". Limited edition of
97 numbered pieces.
75 x 60 x 45cm (29.5 x 23.5 x 17.5in)
Limited edition

Table

"Loop". Low-level plywood coffee table formed in birch
veneer, finished in either walnut or birch.
30 x 60 x 135cm (12 x 23.5 x 53in)
In production

08.06	Barber Osgerby

**Edward Barber and
Jay Osgerby**
167 Trellick Tower
Golborne Road
London W10 5UT
England
Tel: +44 181 960 7928
Fax: +44 181 964 8248

Education
Edward Barber — MA (RCA)
Architecture & Interior
Design, Royal College of Art,
London, England, 1994
Jay Osgerby — MA (RCA)
Architecture & Interior
Design, Royal College of Art,
London, England, 1994

08.07 | **Will Brook** | 64 Carlton Mansions
Holmleigh Road
London N16 5PX
England
Tel: +44 181 802 5049
Fax: +44 171 729 6242
E-mail:
willbrook@hotmail.com

Education
Designing and Making in
Wood, Parnham College,
Dorset, England, 1997

Collections/commissions
Telephone table, Angela
Woods, Professor of Design,
National College of Art and
Design, Dublin, Ireland, 1997
Church pews,
St Michael's Church,
Bridport, Dorset,
England, 1997

Chair
"Alice". Cedar of Lebanon, aeroply, MDF.
90 x 45 x 48cm (35.5 x 17.75 x 19in)
To commission only

08.08 Tony Portus

Cato Studios
133 Sylvia Avenue
Bristol BS3 5BY
England
Tel: +44 117 935 4774
Fax: +44 117 935 4774

Education
Designing and Making in
Wood, Parnham College,
Dorset, England, 1982

Collections/commissions
14 pieces to commission,
private residence,
Sutton Coldfield,
England, 1982-90
Desk and conference table,
Director's office, Bristol,
England, 1994
12 pieces to commission,
private residence,
Manchester, England,
1996-97

Chair
"Cato Rocker". Award-winning handmade rocker in laminated
maple. Other timbers to order. Co-designer Patrick Stronach.
90 x 75 x 90cm (35.5 x 29.5 x 35.5in)
In production

Chairs
"Comb" chair. Structural honeycomb birch plywood and steel.
Chair 79 x 50 x 54cm (31 x 19.5 x 21in)
Armchair 79 x 54 x 54 (31 x 21 x 21in)
In production

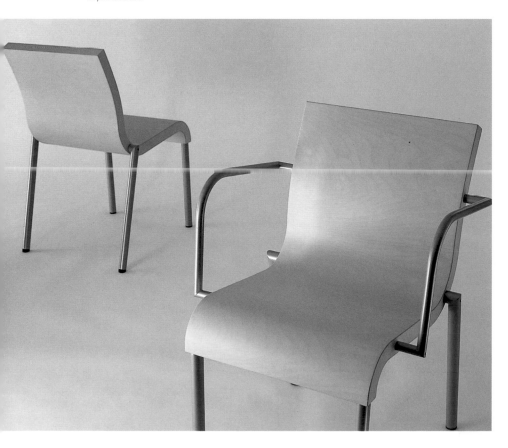

08.09 Byproduct

**James Cannon and
Rob Melville**
Unit 11
Stamford Works
Gillett Street
London N16 8JH
England
Tel: +44 171 923 3430
Fax: +44 171 923 0400

Education
James Cannon — BA
(Hons) Furniture & Related
Product Design,
Ravensbourne College of
Design and Communication,
England, 1994
Rob Melville — BA (Hons)
Industrial Design,
Teesside University,
England, 1985

Collection/commissions
Three Valleys Water plc,
conference room,
Bushey, England, 1997
Lecture and meeting hall,
Crafts Council, London,
England, 1997–98

08.10   Colin Harris Furniture

Colin Harris
56 Crannagh Road
Rathfarnham
Dublin 14
Ireland
Tel: +353 1 490 9370
E-mail:
harriscolin@hotmail.com

Education
BA, BAI, MSc, Trinity College,
Dublin, Ireland, 1995
Designing and Making in
Wood, Parnham College,
Dorset, England, 1997

Collections/commissions
Lounge chair for
Mrs Mimi Lipton,
London, England, 1997
Three tables for
Mr John O'Connor,
Dublin, Ireland, 1998
Display cabinets for new
Computer Science Building,
Trinity College, Dublin,
Ireland, 1998

Table
"Table/Bench". Solid maple top and base. Sections of legs
form simple shape grammar, demonstrating formation of
"table" and "bench" configurations.
Each half of the "Table/Bench" 50 x 60 x 30cm
(20 x 24 x 12in), to make "table" configuration
50 x 60 x 60cm (20 x 24 x 24in) and "bench" configuration
50 x 30 x 120cm (20 x 12 x 48in)
Prototype

Table
Low circular table. Toughened glass,
lacquered MDF, stainless steel brackets.
38 x dia. 110cm (15 x 43.5in)
To commission only

08.11   Cristina Lamíquiz Design

Cristina Lamíquiz
53 Redcliffe Gardens
London SW10 9JJ
England
Tel: +44 171 373 5574
Fax: +44 171 373 5574
E-mail:
cld@c88c.demon.co.uk

Education
BA (Hons) Furniture &
Product Design,
Kingston University,
England, 1991
MA (RCA) Furniture Design,
Royal College of Art,
London, England, 1993

Collections/commissions
"Noodle" stools,
Blackburn collection,
London, England, 1993

Cabinet
"Bongo Drawers". Birch
ply, MDF, painted and
polished finish.
94 x 50 x 35cm
(37 x 19.5 x 13.75in)
To commission only

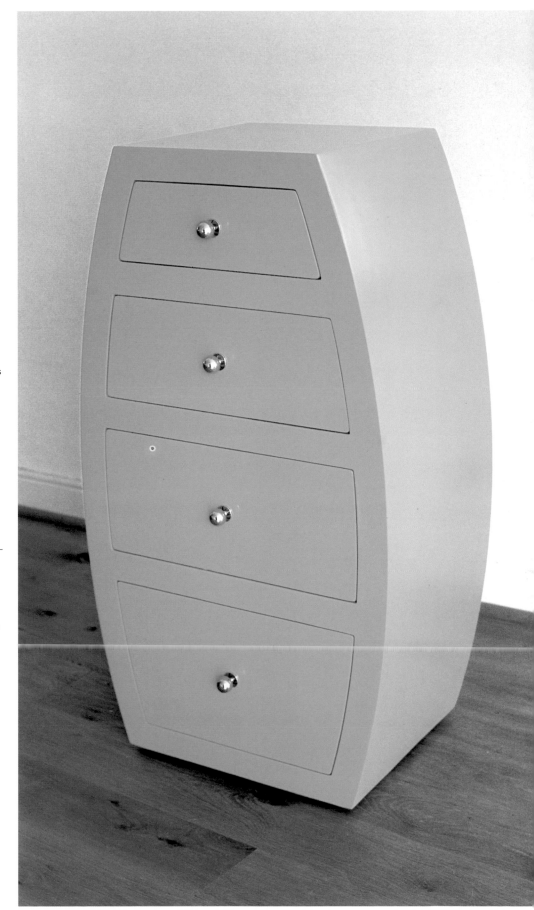

08.12 | Crispin & Gemma
Furniture Design

**Crispin Forster and
Gemma McGregor-Davies**
85 Essox Road
London N1 2SF
England
Tel: +44 171 226 8074
Fax: +44 171 226 8074
E-mail: CrispGem@aol.com

Education
Crispin Forster —
BA (Hons) Fine Art,
Slade School of Fine Art,
University College London,
England, 1993
Gemma McGregor-Davies —
BA (Hons) Fine Art,
Slade School of Fine Art,
University College London,
England, 1993

Collections/commissions
Five designs commissioned
for Liberty's,
London, England, 1997

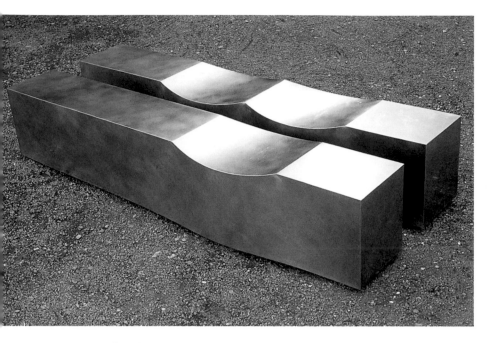

08.13   **Chris Howker Design**   **Chris Howker**
15 Rydens Road
Walton-on-Thames
Surrey KT12 3AA
England
Tel: +44 1932 222529
Fax: +44 1932 222529

Education
BA (Hons) Furniture &
Product Design,
Kingston University,
England, 1995
MA (RCA) Furniture,
Royal College of Art,
London, England, 1997

Benches
"Dip" and "Double Dip". Grooves cut on back of stainless-
steel sheet, then folded along so that dips appear on curved
grooves; process used mostly for small-scale objects such as
jewellery. End panels welded in and adjustable feet and
internal base panel fitted.
230 x 43 x 34cm (90.5 x 17 x 13.25in)
To commission only

08.14   **DJS Design**   **John Sullivan**
20 Myrdle Court
Myrdle Street
London E1 1HP
England
Tel: +44 171 247 5361
Fax: +44 171 247 5361
E-mail: jsullyooo@aol.com

Education
LCF Higher Diploma
Furniture Design &
Production,
London College of Furniture,
England, 1991

Collections/commissions
The Big Breakfast,
Planet 24 Productions for
Channel 4,
London, England, 1995

"FOR AN ITEM OF FURNITURE TO BE SUCCESSFUL IT MUST BE USEFUL AND ADD DELIGHT TO THE LIVES OF THOSE AROUND IT."

08.15 **Fiona Clark Furniture**

Fiona Clark
25 Shacklewell Street
London E2 7EG
England
Tel: +44 171 729 7079

Education
BA (Hons)
Wood/Metal/Plastics/
Ceramics,
Brighton Polytechnic,
England, 1986

Collections/commissions
Furniture and lights, activity
centre, children's section,
The Library, Southampton
Civic Centre, England, 1995
Wall bed, carved English
oak, private commission,
1996
Proscenium arch and box
office area,
Sheringham Little Theatre,
Norfolk, England, 1997

Storage cubes
"Urban Box", part of flexible
storage system. Birch ply,
aluminium laminate, sand-
blasted glass, resin and satin
nickel-plated metal legs.
*(3 x) 40 x 40 x 40cm
(15.75 x 15.75 x 15.75in)
In production*

Sofa
"Lolita". Fully upholstered
wooden frame, polished cast
aluminium feet, 100 per cent
woollen fabric.
*200 x 80 x 90cm
(78.75 x 31.5 x 35.5in)
In production*

Garden seat
"Court Seat" by Christian Gaze. European oak, steam-bent to shape at the corners.
88 x 70 x 152-259cm (34.5 x 27.5 x 60-102in)
In production

08.16	Gaze Burvill

Christian Gaze and Simon Burvill
Plain Farm Old Dairy
East Tisted
Alton
Hampshire GU34 3RT
England
Tel: +44 1420 587467
or +44 1420 588672
Fax: +44 1420 587354

Education
Christian Gaze — Designing and Making in Wood, Parnham College, Dorset, England, 1991
Simon Burvill — BSc (Hons) Engineering, Southampton University, England, 1984
Diploma, Manufacturing in Wood, Hooke Park College, Dorset, England, 1992

08.17	Gabbertas

Mark Gabbertas
Oblique Workshops
Stamford Works
Gillett Street
London N16 8JH
England
Tel: +44 171 503 2112
Fax: +44 171 275 7495
E-mail: gabbers@gabbertas.demon.co.uk

Education
BA (Hons) Political Philosophy and Geography, Durham University, England, 1983

Collections/commissions
Atelier restaurant, London, England, 1996
Allermuir, "30" range of chairs/tables and "Tubby" range of chairs/tables, Darwen, Lancashire, 1997
Head Office, M & C Saatchi, London, England, 1997

Shelving
"Franchi". Flat-pack, self-assembly unit with adjustable shelves. Different curve produced when turned upside down; can be used free-standing as room dividers. Available in birch ply or variety of solid colours, with aluminium detailing.
Large 230 x 80 x 40cm (90.5 x 31.5 x 15.75in)
Small 160 x 70 x 36cm (63 x 27.5 x 14in)
In production

Dining room dresser
Natural and fumed English oak, maple, stainless steel and
toughened glass. Upright beam made with sandwich
construction; invisibly gripping glass shelves inside.
270 x 410 x 50cm (106.25 x 161.5 x 19.75in)
To commission only

08.18 **Christopher Hughes**

3rd Floor, 231 The Vale
Acton
London W3 7QS
England
Tel: +44 181 743 8182
Fax: +44 181 743 8182

Education
HND Spatial Design,
Bournemouth & Poole
College of Art & Design,
England, 1988
Designing and Making in
Wood, Parnham College,
Dorset, England, 1993

Collections/commissions
Box for Christie's
Auctioneers,
South Kensington,
London, England, 1991
"Dylan", English oak and
Welsh slate storage chest,
Willmott/Poe,
private collection,
Boston, USA, 1993

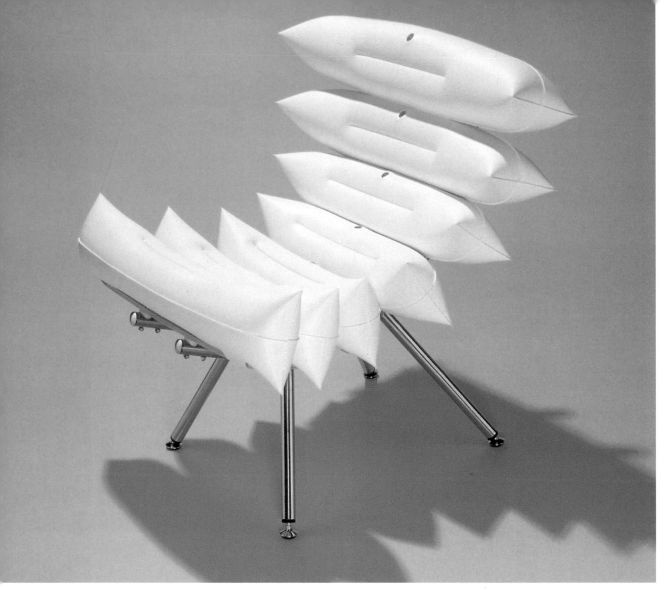

Chair
Single lounge chair.
High-frequency welded
inflatables, steel tube
chrome-plated, wood.
*70 x 75 x 60cm
(27.5 x 29.5 x 23.5in)
In production*

| 08.19 | Inflate | **Nick Crosbie,
Mark Sodeau and
Nitzan Yaniv** |

3rd Floor, 5 Old Street
London EC1V 9HL
England
Tel: +44 171 251 5453
Fax: +44 171 250 0311

Education
Nick Crosbie — MA (RCA)
Industrial Design,
Royal College of Art,
London, England, 1995
Mark Sodeau — BEng (Hons)
Aeronautical Engineering,
City University,
London, England, 1993
Nitzan Yaniv —
LLB (Hons) Law,
University of Birmingham,
England, 1993

08.20   **Walter Jack**

56 William Street
Totterdown
Bristol BS3 4TY
England
Tel: +44 117 939 3336
or +44 117 909 9329

Education
BA (Hons) 3D Design,
University of West England,
Bristol, England, 1981

Collections/commissions
"East/West" seat for Bristol
City Museum,
England, 1996
Seating for main hall,
Royal Museum for Scotland,
Edinburgh, Scotland, 1997
"Sheltered" seat for
Parrett Sculpture Trail,
Burrowbridge, Somerset,
England, 1997

Seating
"Whalebone Seats". Oak and powder-coated steel seats in pairs, fitted with rollers for moving.
200 x 180 x 600cm (78.75 x 71 x 236.25in)
To commission only

Table
"MDF storage table" constructed using KD fittings. The coloured MDF table lids are dyed using fabric dye.
108 x 55 x 32cm (42.5 x 21.75 x 12.5in)
In production

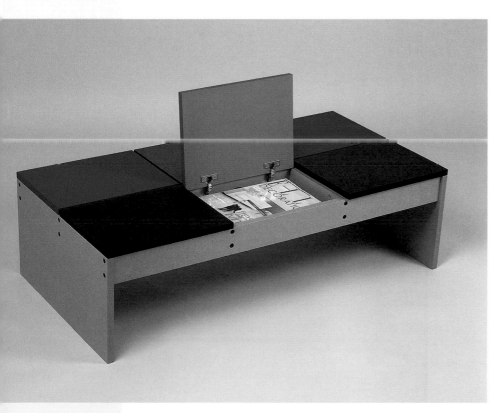

08.21   **Ray Davies**

39 Grove Lane
Chalfont St Peter
Buckinghamshire SL9 9LL
England
Tel: +44 1753 887964

Education
BA (Hons) Furniture Design &
Craftsmanship,
Buckinghamshire College,
High Wycombe, England,
1997

08.22   **JAM Design & Communications**

Jamie Anley, Astrid Zala and Matthieu Paillard
Top Floor, 1 Goodsway
Kings Cross
London NW1 1UR
England
Tel: +44 171 278 5567
Fax: +44 171 278 3263

Education
Jamie Anley —BSc Arch,
Bartlett School of
Architecture,
University College of London,
England, 1995
Astrid Zala —
BA (Hons) Fine Art,
Goldsmiths College,
London, England, 1991
Matthieu Paillard —
Architectural Apprentice,
Valfort Design, Nice, France,
1993

Collections/commissions
Manchester City Arts
Council, permanent
collection, England, 1997
Norman bar/restaurant,
Leeds, England, 1997
Guggenheim Museum,
SoHo, New York, USA, 1998

Storage cabinet
"Robo-stacker". Whirlpool top-loading washing machine
drums with metal base and glass top.
126 x dia. 47cm (49.5 x 18.5in)
In production

Table

"Britten" extending table. Solid American oak, extendable with two leaves hung under the top. Adjustable to three different sizes of table top, seating when closed 4/6 people, open with one leaf 8/10 people, and open with both leaves 10/12 people.
75 x 95 x 190-290cm (29.5 x 37.5 x 75-114.25in)
In production

08.24 Matthew Hilton **c/o SCP Limited**
135–139 Curtain Road
London EC2A 3BX
England
Tel: +44 171 739 1869
Fax: +44 171 729 4224
E-mail:
scp@online.rednet.co.uk

Education
BA (Hons) Furniture Design,
Kingston University,
England, 1980

Collections/commissions
Domestic and contract furniture for Driade SpA, Piacenza, Italy, 1997–98 Complete range of laser cut/folded stainless steel, nickel plated, and aluminium door handles, for Handles and Fittings, Hertfordshire, England, 1997–98 Injection-moulded translucent polypropylene clock for Authentics, Holzgerlingen, Germany, 1998

08.23 Katie Walker Furniture **Katie Walker**
Cox Farm Studios
Dorking Road
Warnham
West Sussex RH12 3RZ
England
Tel: +44 1403 211323
Fax: +44 1403 211323

Education
BA (Hons) Furniture & Product Design, Ravensbourne College of Design and Communication, Kent, England, 1991 MA (RCA) Furniture Design, Royal College of Art, London, England, 1993

Collections/commissions
Public seating for the Royal Parks Department, Department of National Heritage, London, England, 1993 Boardroom table and chairs, Prince's Trust Headquarters, London, England, 1996 Console table for Hove Museum and Art Gallery, South East Arts and Craft Collection, East Sussex, England, 1997

Table

Breakfast table. Solid sycamore top with laminated sycamore underframe.
73.5 x 180 x 91cm (29 x 71 x 36in)
To commission only

08.25 | **Jyri Kermik** | 6 Bankside Close, Park Hill
Carshalton Beeches
Surrey SM5 3SB
England
Tel: +44 181 647 0436
Fax: +44 181 647 0436
E-mail: kermik@lineone.net

Education
MPhil (RCA) Furniture
Design, Royal College of Art,
London, England, 1994

Collections/commissions
The Estonian Ambassador's
Residence, London,
England, 1995

Chair
"Moon-Chair". Plywood, tubular steel frame. Manufactured by
Avarte Oy, Finland.
75 x 51 x 51cm (29.5 x 20 x 20in)
In production

08.26 | **Kiosk and Made of Waste** | **Jane Atfield**
244 Grays Inn Road
London WC1X 8JR
England
Tel: +44 171 833 0018
Fax: +44 171 833 0018

Education
BA (Hons) Architecture,
School of Architecture,
Polytechnic of Central
London, England, 1987
MA (RCA) Furniture Design,
Royal College of Art,
London, England, 1992

Collections/commissions
Indoor and outdoor
tables/chairs, Newbury Arts
Centre and District Council,
Berkshire, England, 1997
Victoria & Albert Museum,
permanent collection,
London, England, 1997
Die Neue Sammlung
collection, Munich,
Germany, 1997

Tables
Made of waste recycled plastic, high-density polyethylene.
35 x 30 x 30cm (13.75 x 12 x 12in)
In production

08.27 | Robert Kilvington

Charles Bottom Cross
Brayford
Barnstaple EX32 7PY
England
Tel: +44 1598 760356
Fax: +44 1598 760356
E-mail:
kilvington@compuserve.com

Education
Designing and Making in
Wood, Parnham College,
Dorset, England, 1991
MA (RCA) Furniture Design,
Royal College of Art,
London, England, 1994

Collections/commissions
"Crossing the line", gateway
sculpture to Tilsley Athletics
Park, commissioned by the
Vale of White Horse District
Council, Abingdon,
Oxfordshire, England, 1997
Stacking contract chair,
commissioned by Ness
Furniture Limited, Croxdale,
Durham, England, 1997
art.tm gallery seating (six
benches), commissioned
jointly by art.tm gallery,
Inverness, Scotland, and
The Edward Marshall Trust,
Surrey, England, 1998

Bench
"Wave". Constructed from solid oak blocks and available in
single-, two- and three-seater versions.
Single seat 45 x 60 x 36cm (17.5 x 23.5 x 14in)
Two-seater 45 x 120 x 36cm (17.5 x 47 x 14in)
Three-seater 45 x 180 x 36cm (17.5 x 71 x 14in)
To commission only

08.28 | **Phil Lardner** | Oblique Workshops
Stamford Works
Gillett Street
London N16 8JH
England
Tel: +44 171 503 2116
Fax: +44 171 275 7495

Education
BA (Hons) Furniture Design &
Craftsmanship,
Buckinghamshire College,
High Wycombe,
England, 1995

Cabinet
"Flex". 2mm birch-faced
plywood and steel pins.
Machine-routed components
slot together to make
carcass and drawers.
Winner of the 1995 Gordon
Russell DIA Award.
Nine-drawer cabinet
108 x 40 x 34.5cm
(42.5 x 15.75 x 13.5in)
Three-drawer cabinet
42 x 40 x 34.5cm
(16.5 x 15.75 x 13.5in)
In production

Armchair/table
"Armchair=Table" by Shin Azumi. This armchair can be changed into a table with simple and smooth action. This provides extra table surface when needed, otherwise it is an armchair in a living room. It is made from Maple veneered MDF, solid maple and steel tube.
Chair - 83 x 58 x 62cm (32.5 x 23 x 24.5in)
Table - 70 x 58 x 90cm (27.5 x 23 x 35.5in)
In production

08.30 | **Azumi's**

Shin & Tomoko Azumi
Ground Floor
953 Finchley Road
London NW11 7PE
England
Tel:+44 181 731 7496
Fax:+44 181 731 7496

Education
Shin Azumi - BA (Hons) Product Design, Kyoto City University of Art, Japan, 1989
MA (RCA) Industrial Design, Royal College of Art, London, England, 1994
Tomoko Azumi - BA (Hons) Environmental Design, Kyoto City University of Art, Japan, 1989
MA (RCA) Furniture Design, Royal College of Art, London, England, 1995

Collections/commissions
Crafts Council, permanent collection, London, England, 1995
Geffrye Design Museum collection, London, England, 1996
Victoria & Albert Museum, permanent collection, London, England, 1997

08.29 | **Lime Design**

Jonathan Hoad
121 Glyn Road
London E5 0JA
England
Tel: +44 181 985 6733
Fax: +44 181 985 6733
E-mail: lime@dircon.co.uk

Education
BA (Hons) 3D Design/Furniture, Buckinghamshire College, High Wycombe, England, 1991

Collections/commissions
Seating for The Big Issue, London, England, 1994
Bed, "The Sea Change", Winchester Pictures Film Company, London, England, 1997

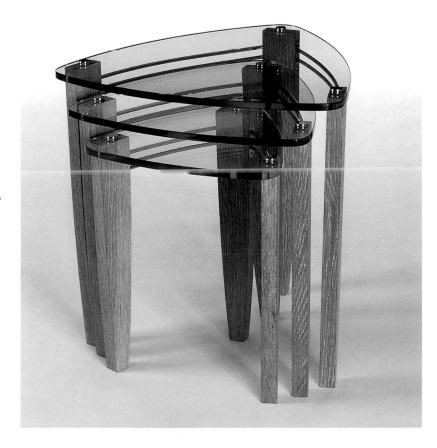

Nest of tables
"Three 3's". Glass, chrome fittings and fumed, limed oak legs.
50 x 52 x 52cm (19.5 x 20.5 x 20.5in)
In production

08.31 | **Mark Bond Design**

Mark Bond
Prism Design Studio
38 Grosvenor Gardens
London SW1W 0EB
England
Tel: +44 171 730 3011
Fax: +44 171 730 3011

Education
MA (RCA) Furniture Design,
Royal College of Art,
London, England, 1994

Collections/commissions
Tableware, Habitat Products,
London, England, 1994–98
The Design Museum shop,
café and Review Gallery,
London, England, 1997
Design of reception interior
and accompanying furniture
(tables, coffee tables),
CIA Media,
London, England, 1997–98

Extending table
"4 Times Table". Beech table
top, mild steel legs.
73 x 80 x 160cm
(29 x 31.5 x 63in)
In production

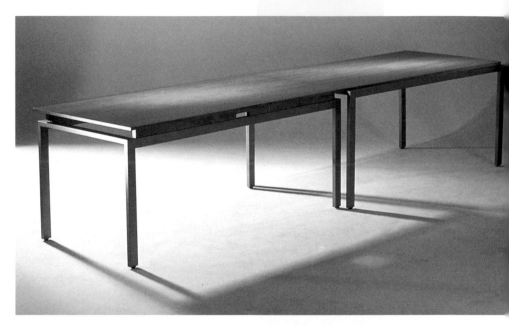

Sofa
Blue upholstered sofa.
76 x 170 x 82.5cm
(29.5 x 67 x 32.5in)
In production

08.32 | **Alex Macdonald**

25 Shacklewell Street
Shoreditch
London E2 7EG
England
Tel: +44 171 729 7079
Fax: +44 171 729 6242

Education
Designing and Making in
Wood, Parnham College,
Dorset, England, 1985

| 08.33 | **Angel Monzon** | 114 Kensington Park Road
London W11 2PW
England
Tel: +44 171 727 5174
Fax: +44 171 229 8377
E-mail: a.monzon@rca.ac.uk |

Education
BA (Hons) Furniture Design,
Kingston University,
England, 1996

"I BELIEVE THAT METAL
CAN BE USED
IN A DOMESTIC CONTEXT,
BEING BOTH STURDY
AND PRACTICAL
YET STILL ELEGANT AND
COMFORTING
WHEN WELL DESIGNED."

Storage unit
Part of "Roundsquare" collection. Powder-coated sheet metal
and stained cherry wood, with two round corners challenging
two square corners.
Storage unit with two vertical divisions
48 x 99 x 33cm (19 x 39 x 13in)
In production

Chair
"MY001 Café Chair". Tubular steel frame, silver polyester turned aluminium feet, painted beech plywood seat, designed for TYMC.
48 x 52 x 75cm (19 x 20.5 x 29.5in)
In production

08.34 MY-022

Michael Young
c/o TYMC London
Unit 3a
101 Farm Lane
London SW6 1QJ
England
Tel: +44 171 610 0799
Fax: +44 171 386 9584
E-mail: tymc@dial.pipex.com

Education
BA (Hons) Furniture Design,
Kingston University, England,
1992

Collections/commissions
Mid-90s Modern Furniture
Collection for E&Y Ltd,
Tokyo, Japan, 1995
Design Museum,
permanent collection,
London, England, 1996
Atelier des Enfants,
Centre Pompidou,
Paris, France, 1996

Sofa
"MY003 Magazine". Two-seat sofa designed for TYMC. Wooden frame with fire-retardant polyurethane foam. Brushed aluminium legs, upholstered white vinyl fabric.
64 x 62 x 142cm (25.25 x 24.5 x 56in)
In production

Bar stool
"Luna". Die-cast aluminium
seat and foot ring with
aluminium tube legs.
Both high and low versions
flat-pack.
Manufactured by Allermuir
Contract Furniture Ltd.,
Darwen, Lancashire,
England.
75 x dia. 47cm
(29.5 x 18.5in)
In production

| 08.35 | Amos Marchant | 95–97 Redchurch Street
London E2 7DJ
England
Tel: +44 171 613 0202
Fax: +44 171 613 2181

Education
BA (Hons) Furniture &
Product Design,
Kingston University,
England, 1987
MA Design Studies,
Central St Martins College of
Art & Design,
London, England, 1996

Collections/commissions
"Luna" range of aluminium
indoor/outdoor bar furniture,
Allermuir Contract Furniture
Ltd., Darwen, Lancashire,
England, 1996-97

08.36 **McDaniel Woolf**

Richard Woolf
18 Mariner Gardens
Richmond
Surrey TW10 7UT
England
Tel: +44 181 332 1981
Fax: +44 181 332 1251

Education
BA (Hons) Industrial Design,
Dc Montfort University,
Leicestershire, England,
1984
Diploma Architecture,
Kingston University,
England, 1997

Collections/commissions
Store interior, Muji,
Oxford Street, London,
England, 1997
Englender Furniture
collection, Derbyshire,
England, 1997
Office interior, Hilson Moran,
Farnborough, England, 1998

Wall-mounted shelves
"Duo". Rosewood veneer.
100 x 100 x 30cm
(39.5 x 39.5 x 12in)
In production

Tables
Collection of tables for
Japanese retailer Muji, for
home or light commercial
use. Beech timber frames
and lippings with high-
pressure laminate tops and
industrial aluminium casters.
Designed by McDaniel Woolf
and manufactured by
Englender Furniture,
Derbyshire, England.
Table 75 x 150 x 72cm
(29.5 x 58 x 28in)
Low table 95 x 60 x 40cm
(37 x 23 x 16in)
Side table 45 x 45 x 60cm
(18 x 18 x 23in)
In production

08.37 **Michael Sodeau Partnership**

**Michael Sodeau and
Lisa Giuliani**
24 Rosebery Avenue
London EC1R 4SX
England
Tel: +44 171 837 2343
Fax: +44 171 837 2343

Education
Michael Sodeau —
BA (Hons) Product Design,
Central St Martins College
of Art & Design,
London, England, 1994

Chair
"Pom Pom" bean bag.
Mongolian lambskin (natural
or dyed colours), leather
base, cotton lined, poly-bean
filled sack, hand-stitched.
*90 x dia. 100cm
(35.5 x 39.5in)
To commission only*

"THE FUTURE'S
BRIGHT—
THE FUTURE'S
PRECIOUS."

08.38	Precious McBane

**Meriel Scott and
Evlynn Smith**
112 Aberfeldy House
John Ruskin Street
London SE5 0XJ
England
Tel: +44 171 735 5140
Fax: +44 171 735 5140

Education
Meriel Scott — BA (Hons)
Fine Art Sculpture,
Central St Martins College
of Art & Design,
London, England, 1991
Evlynn Smith — BA (Hons)
Fine Art Sculpture,
Central St Martins College
of Art & Design,
London, England, 1993

Collections/commissions
Seating installation for Lux
Cinema, Hoxton Square,
London, England, 1997
ISPI Urban Equipment
(collaboration with
Juggernaut),
sunglasses showroom,
Covent Garden,
London, England, 1998

08.39 | Malig | **Michael Malig**
162 Wynford Road
London N1 9SW
England
Tel: +44 171 833 9457
Fax: +44 171 833 9457

Education
BA (Hons) Ravensbourne
College of Design and
Communication, Kent,
England, 1991
MA (RCA) Furniture,
Royal College of Art,
London, England, 1994

Collections/commissions
art.tm gallery seating and
table, commissioned jointly
by art.tm gallery, Inverness,
Scotland, and The Edward
Marshall Trust, Surrey,
England, 1998
Seating, Walsall Leather
Museum, England, 1998

"MY APPROACH
IS HUMANISTIC,
DESIGNING AND
DEVELOPING
INNOVATIVE OBJECTS
AND FOCUSING ON
HOW OBJECTS
OFFER
EXPERIENCE."

Stool
"Little Tail". Stacking stool
(stacks 20). Coated
plywood, leather and steel.
*32 x 32 x 43cm
(12 x 12 x 17in)
In production*

| 08.40 | Niki | **Niki Bolza** |

57a Archel Road
West Kensington
London W14 9QJ
England
Tel: +44 171 431 5070
Fax: +44 171 431 5070

Education
BA (Hons) Sculpture,
Chelsea College of Art,
London, England, 1995

Collections/commission
Scenery/stage set and
furniture, Smirnoff Vodka
commercial for
Lowe Howard Spink,
London, England, 1997
The Bowes Museum,
Durham, England, 1998
Commission by Set Pieces
for "Balance of the Force",
"Star Wars" film, 1998

Chair
"Spike" chair. Chromed steel
and yew wood.
75 x 30 x 30cm
(29.5 x 12 x 12in)
To commission only

Paul Gower

4 Manor Buildings
North Perrott
Crewkerne
Somerset TA18 7ST
England
Tel: +44 1460 75959
Fax: +44 1460 75959

Education
Designing and Making in
Wood, Parnham College,
Dorset, England, 1992

Collections/commissions
Reception furniture, Credit
Suisse Bank, Canary Wharf,
London, England, 1994
Bedroom furniture,
Saudi Royal Family
(Gordon Lindsay Design),
London, England, 1997
Reception furniture, Gordon
Lindsay Design offices,
London, England, 1998

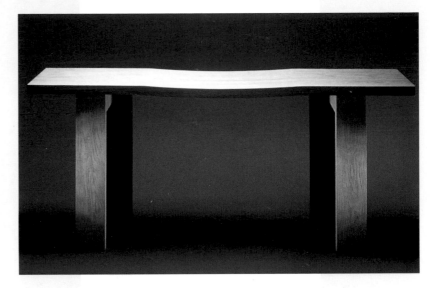

Table
"Square Peg". Solid
bleached English oak.
*73 x 60 x 170cm
(28.75 x 23.5 x 63.5in)
To commission only*

Bed and cabinet
"Waffle" bed and "El-Chico"
cabinet. Bed in birch ply with
hollow-core construction.
Cabinet in maple, MDF and
aluminium.
*Bed 240 x 150 x 120cm
(95 x 59 x 47in)
Cabinet 92 x 35 x 35cm
(36 x 13.75 x 13.75in)
To commission only*

"I COMBINE COLOUR,
MATERIALS AND SHAPE TO PROVIDE
FUNCTIONAL FURNITURE
WITH A STRONG SENSE OF HUMOUR."

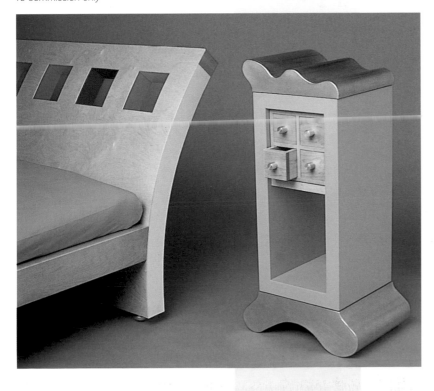

Michael Matthews

9 Worthy Lane
Winchester
Hampshire SO23 7AB
England
Tel: +44 1962 852254
Fax: +44 1962 852254
E-mail:
peagreen@easynet.co.uk

Education
BEng Electrical Engineering,
Trent Polytechnic,
Nottingham, England, 1989
Designing and Making in
Wood, Parnham College,
Dorset, England, 1996

Collections/commissions
Chapel furniture for
Bridport Community
Hospital,
Dorset, England, 1996

Chair
"Rad". Cherry or pear wood
and satin-chromed steel.
68 x 53 x 40cm
(26.75 x 21 x 15.75in)
To commission only

08.43   **Simon Pengelly**   Prism Studio
38 Grosvenor Gardens
London SW1W 0EB
England
Tel: +44 171 730 3211
Fax: +44 171 730 3211

Education
BA (Hons) 3D Design,
Furniture & Related
Products,
Kingston Polytechnic,
England, 1988

Collections/commissions
Numerous pieces of furniture
designed for Habitat, selling
in UK, France, Italy,
Germany, Spain and
franchises worldwide
Three products currently
being prototyped for
production, Cappellini SpA,
Arosio, Italy, 1998
Chair currently in
development,
Gordon Russell, Broadway,
Worcestershire, England,
1998

Occasional table
"Tam". MDF, laminate, pear
veneer and solids. Opening
solid pear wood tambour
reveals storage space
inside table.
38 x 59 x 120cm
(15 x 23.25 x 47.25in)
To commission only

Shelving unit
"U2". Cherry wood and
powder-coated steel.
180 x 33.5 x 120cm
(71 x 13.25 x 47.25in)
Prototype, in production by
end 1998

08.44 | **Stephen Philips** | 52 Park Street
Thame
Oxfordshire OX9 3HS
England
Tel: +44 1844 214897
Fax: +44 1844 214897

Education
BA (Hons) Furniture &
Product Design,
Buckinghamshire College,
High Wycombe,
England, 1992

Collections/commissions
Seating commissioned by
Hampshire Architects
School,
Eastleigh, England, 1994
Interactive reception area for
In Real Life, design
competition winner,
London, England, 1996

Chair
"Open-Ended" chair. Steel tube, polyurethane, zip-on
neoprene covers, upholstered seat, backrest and armrest.
73 x 40 x 55cm (28.5 x 15.5 x 21.5in)
In production

Mobile office
"Homer". Steel and aluminium carcass, laminated
beech tray, moulded ABS base and top.
67 x 59 x 38.5cm (26.5 x 23.25 x 15in)
In production

08.45 | **Pearson Lloyd
Design Partnership** | **Luke Pearson and
Tom Lloyd**
39-41 Folgate Street
London E1 6BX
England
Tel: +44 171 377 0560
Fax: +44 171 247 4317
E-mail:
design@pearsonlloyd.demon.
co.uk

Education
Luke Pearson — MA (RCA)
Furniture Design,
Royal College of Art,
London, England, 1993
Tom Lloyd — MA (RCA)
Industrial Design,
Royal College of Art,
London, England, 1993

Collections/commissions
Interior for
Duffer of St. George,
London, England, 1997

08.47 | **Nicholas Pryke Productions**

Nicholas Pryke
No.1 Kingston Mews
Oxford OX2 6RJ
England
Tel: +44 1865 310400
Fax: +44 1865 316300
E-mail:
nic.pryke@npproductions.
demon.co.uk

Education
Designing and Making in
Wood, Parnham College,
Dorset, England, 1998

Collections/commissions
Interior of café, reception
and shop,
Nottingham Castle Museum,
Nottingham, England, 1993
Furniture for reception,
Virgin Interactive
Entertainment,
London, England, 1995
Interior of Patient Resource
Centre,
Queen Elizabeth Hospital,
Birmingham, England, 1998

Table
Low table. Solid oak.
40 x 70 x 120cm (15.75 x 27.5 x 47.25in)
To commission only

Low table
Occasional table with solid steel bar structure, powder-coated
in white or grey, toughened glass top.
42.5 x 100 x 100cm (16.75 x 39.5 x 39.5in)
In production

08.46 | **Konstantin Grcic**

c/o SCP Limited
135–139 Curtain Road
London EC2A 3BX
England
Tel: +44 171 739 1869
Fax: +44 171 729 4224
E-mail:
scp@online.rednet.co.uk

Education
MA (RCA) Furniture,
Royal College of Art,
London, England, 1990

Collections/commissions
Authentics GmbH,
Holzgerlingen, Germany
Driade SpA,
Fossadello de Caorso, Italy
Cappellini SpA, Arosio, Italy

08.48 | **Procter-Rihl**

Fernando Rihl
190c Royal College Street
London NW1 9NN
England
Tel: +44 171 284 0248
Fax: +44 171 916 1517
E-mail:
cprocter@dircon.co.uk

Education
AA Graduate Diploma,
Architectural Association,
London, England, 1993

Collections/commissions
Acrylic screens, Joyce shop,
Hong Kong, China, 1996
Exhibition stand for
Blueprint Magazine,
London, England, 1997
Nail bar, Colette shop,
Paris, France, 1997

"THE STRENGTH OF BRITISH DESIGN RELIES ON ITS ECLECTICISM AND ANARCHISM WHICH WILL CONTINUE IN THE FUTURE."

Shelving system
"Topo Shelving". Flat-pack
system in birch plywood and
blue translucent plastic
uprights and shelves,
assembled randomly by
user. Undulating three-
dimensional front face,
defining prismatic structure.
*200 x 200 x 34cm
(78.75 x 78.75 x 14in)
Prototype*

08.49 | **Sam Design Limited**

Simon Maidment
Basement
108 Huddleston Road
Islington
London N7 0EG
England
Tel: +44 171 272 8294
Fax: +44 171 272 8294

Education
MA (RCA) Furniture,
Royal College of Art,
London, England, 1992

Collections/commissions
"Baby Tambour" chair,
Vitra Design Museum,
permanent collection,
Weil am Rhein,
Germany, 1998

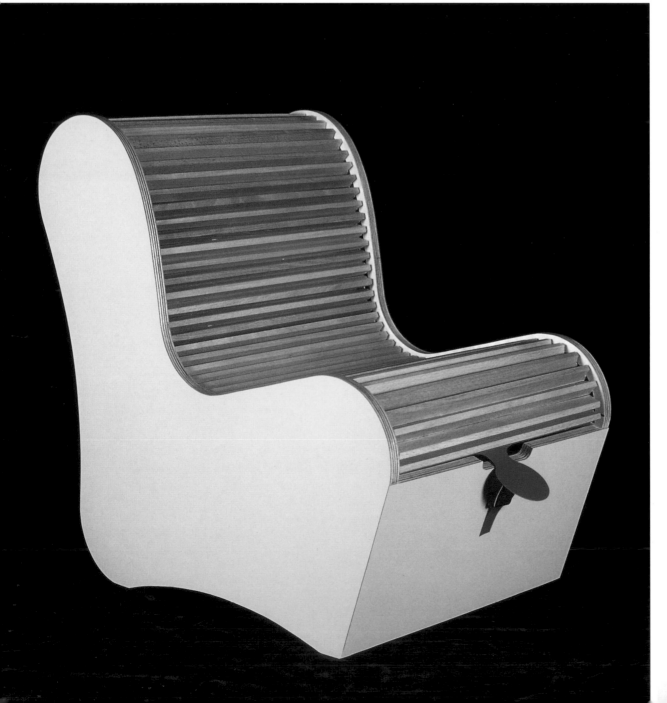

Chair
"Baby Tambour" chair.
Beech hardwood tambour,
birch ply carcass, plastic
laminate finish.
42 x 38 x 36cm
(16.5 x 15 x 14in)
To commission only

08.51 | **Roy Sant** | 67 Wilberforce Road
Finsbury Park
London N4 2SP
England
Tel: +44 171 704 1592
Fax: +44 171 704 1592

Education
BA (Hons) 3D Design/
Furniture, Leeds
Metropolitan University,
England, 1995

Collections/commissions
"Divider" series storage
system commissioned by
Beams Co. Ltd,
Tokyo, Japan, 1997

Shelving
From large "Divider" series. MDF with laminate and solid
beech edging and CNC folded steel supports.
Basic unit 52 x 37 x 122cm (20.5 x 14.5 x 48in).
Additional levels can be attached for extra storage with each
level, adding 39cm (15.5in) to height.
To commission only

Table
Welded aluminium and anodized aluminium
laminate top.
200 x 100 x 72cm (79 x 39 x 29in)
To commission only

08.50 | **Regitze Bondesen** | 92 Sandbrook Road
London N16 0SP
England
Tel: +44 171 249 6580
Fax: +44 171 249 6580

Education
BA (Hons) Furniture Design
and Technology,
London Guildhall University,
England, 1993

Collections/commissions
Restaurant lighting, The
Lansdowne, Primrose Hill,
London, England, 1995
Dining room, 18-seater table
and matching mirror,
private client,
London, England, 1997
Dining table, half indoors and
half outdoors, private client,
Copenhagen, Denmark,
1998

08.52 **Caius John Shaw**

25 Main Road
Long Hanborough
near Witney
Oxfordshire OX8 3BD
England
Tel: +44 1993 881647
Fax: +44 1993 883669
E-mail: caius@udirect.co.uk

Education
MA (RCA) Furniture,
Royal College of Art,
London, England, 1996

Collections/commissions
Ceiling light installation,
private client,
London, England, 1997
Writing desk,
private client,
London, England, 1998

Desk (stool and lamp)
Sloping writing desk and lamp with tilting stool. Made from
solid maple timber and veneer.
Table 69–81 x 60 x 120cm (27–32 x 23.5 x 47.25in)
Lamp height 150cm (59in)
To commission only

Shelving
"Plug It" shelving environment.
Back panels 160 x 60cm (63 x 23.5in)
Boxes 52 x 22 x 25cm (20.5 x 8.5 x 9.75in)
Prototype, in production by end 1998

08.53 **El Ultimo Grito**

Roberto Feo
26 Northfield House
Frensham Street
London SE15 6TL
England
Tel: +44 171 732 6614
Fax: +44 171 732 6614

Education
MA (RCA) Furniture,
Royal College of Art,
London, England, 1997

Collections/commissions
Light "Don't Run We Are
Your Friends", Review
Gallery, Design Museum,
London, England, 1997

Andrew Stafford
95–97 Redchurch Street
London E2 7DJ
England
Tel: +44 171 613 0054
Fax: +44 171 613 2181
E-mail: staf@shire.u-net.com

Education
DATEC Diploma Product
Design, West Sussex
College of Design,
Worthing, England, 1984
BA (Hons) Furniture &
Product Design,
Kingston Polytechnic,
England, 1987

Collections/commissions
Sideboard, bed and table for
private residence,
London, England, 1996–97
Benches, commissioned by
Allford Hall Monaghan Morris
Architects
for Broadgate Club West,
London, England, 1997
Interior commissioned by
design consultancy
Brinkworth, for "Only"
womenswear (retail outlet),
London, England, 1997

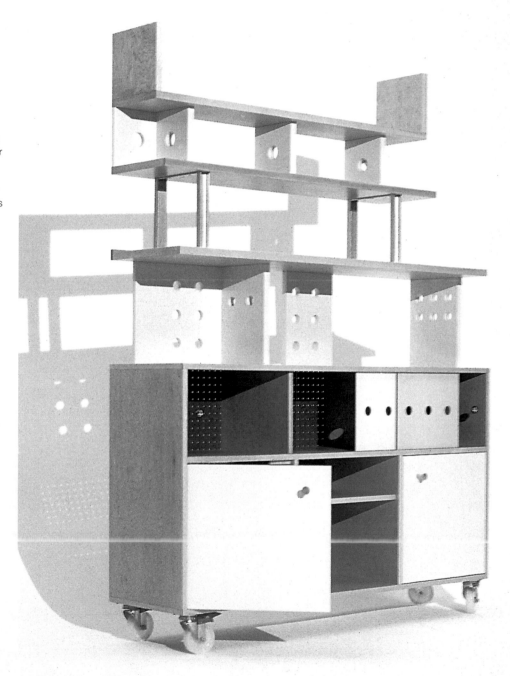

Sideboard
"Barry Island". Maple,
lacquered MDF, perforated
hardboard, glass and
zinc-plated steel.
160 x 40 x 160cm
(63 x 16 x 63in)
To commission only

Chair
"Rhyme" chair. Laminated curved seat and back on a solid wooden framework with laminated back legs in pear wood.
43 x 45 x 88cm
(17 x 17.75 x 34.5in)
To commission only

08.55 | Stemmer & Sharp

Andrea Stemmer
2 Wren Street
London WC1X 0HA
England
Tel: +44 171 503 2105
Fax: +44 171 275 7495

Education
Designing and Making in Wood, Parnham College, Dorset, England, 1989

Collections/commissions
Furniture for three executive offices, Clinic Catering Services, Düsseldorf, Germany, 1995
Refurbishment of entrance hall, comprising reception desk, sales counter, sales area, shelving and storage cabinets, postcard racks and notice boards,
Hove Museum & Art Gallery, England, 1996
Garden furniture comprising four chairs, two benches and three tables,
M and Mme Malouf, Antibes, France, 1997

Garden furniture
"Jekyell" garden table and benches. Slatted asymmetric top on traditionally constructed frame with curved bottom rail. Solid oak benches (one straight and one curved) follow outline of table.
Table 180 x 80 x 73cm
(70.75 x 31.5 x 28.75in)
Benches 180 x 40 x 45cm
(70.75 x 15.75 x 17.75in)
To commission only

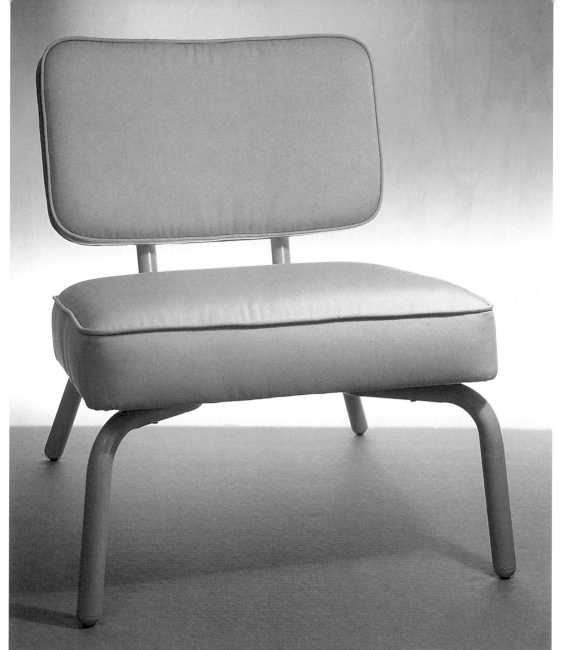

Reception/lounge chair
"Havana". Powder-coated
tubular metal frame with
interchangeable upholstered
panels.
Manufactured by Ness
Furniture Limited,
Durham, England.
70 x 62 x 68cm
(27.5 x 24.5 x 26.75in)
In production

08.56 | Studio Delo

Nick Delo
3rd Floor
5 Old Street
London EC1V 9HL
England
Tel: +44 171 250 0685
Fax: +44 171 250 0685

Education
BA (Hons) Product Design,
Central St Martins College
of Art & Design,
London, England, 1994

Collections/commissions
Shop interior, trade show
stand and office for
Boxfresh (streetwear
manufacturer/retailer),
London, England, 1997-98
Interior proposals, British
Council information centre,
Brussels, Belgium, 1998

Stacking chair

"Ed's Stack" chair by Pat Booth and Nina Moeller. Hot-pressed laminations of wood, folded and extruded aluminium and rubber dip-moulded feet. Lightweight, stacks vertically upwards, and available in various finishes.
40 x 40 x 87.5cm
(15.75 x 15.75 x 34.5in)
In production

Table

"Yemeni" table by Pat Booth. Hinge made from woven stainless steel springs, allowing table to extend from space-saving desk or console table to eight-seater boardroom/dining room table. Also available as six-seater. Usually made in cherry, although other hard woods possible, and flat-packs.
Eight-seater 75 x 92 x 200cm (29.5 x 36.25 x 78.75in)
Six-seater 75 x 82 x 150cm (29.5 x 32.25 x 59in)
In production

"PLEASURE MEETS FUNCTION, STRIVING FOR SIMPLICITY. MATERIALS EXCITE SOLUTIONS."

08.57 | **Studio Kew Bridge**

Pat Booth and Nina Moeller
Steam Museum
Green Dragon Lane
Brentford
Middlesex TW8 0EN
England
Tel: +44 171 602 9344
or +44 1932 827447
Fax: +44 171 602 9344
or +44 1932 827447

Education

Pat Booth — Mixed Media, Banff Centre, Alberta, Canada, 1982
Cabinet Making, London College of Furniture, England, 1989
Workshop, Hooke Park (Parnham Trust), Dorset, England, 1991
Nina Moeller — Apprenticeship in cabinetmaking in small firm in Bremerhaven, Germany, 1984-87
Designing and Making in Wood, Parnham College, Dorset, England, 1989

Collections/commissions

Oak and leather upholstered stacking chairs and bar tables, private function room, Ivy Restaurant, London, England, 1994
Large reception desk, Independent Living Centre, Essex County Council, Bishops Stortford, England, 1996
Boardroom table for British Consulate General, Düsseldorf, Germany, 1997

Sofa

"Kama". Upholstered sofa with multi-depth curved seat, for creating intimate or formal environments. Shape of back combined with seat allows for upright or relaxed seating positions. Individual components with one, two or no arms, or to create bench, and on large scale as integral part of sofa system layout. Upholstered hardwood timber frame with die-cast aluminium legs.
Produced by Aram Designs Limited, London, England.
85 x 85 x 160cm (33.5 x 33.5 x 63in)
In production

08.58 | Studio Orange

Rock Galpin
70–72 Kingsland Road
London E2 8DP
England
Tel: +44 171 684 9422
Fax: +44 171 684 9423

Education
BA (Hons) Product Design,
3D Design, Wood, Metal &
Plastics,
University of
Wolverhampton,
England, 1988
MA Industrial Design,
Central St Martins College
of Art & Design,
London, England, 1990

Collections/commissions
Sofa design and range of
tables,
Aram Designs Limited,
London, England, 1996
New household product
collections for
Authentics Limited,
London, England, 1996-98
Seven presenter tables
including two "Chameleon"
tables, *The Big Breakfast*,
Planet 24 Productions for
Channel 4,
London, England, 1993–97

Bench
Laminated birch plywood.
100 x 450 x 70cm
(39.5 x 177 x 27.5in)
To commission only

Bench
Cast terrazzo.
100 x 220 x 70cm
(39.5 x 86.5 x 27.5in)
Prototype

"IN MY STUDIO'S WORK
I AM TRYING TO BLUR
THE EDGES BETWEEN
ART, DESIGN AND
ARCHITECTURE."

08.59 Thomas Heatherwick Studio

Thomas Heatherwick
129 Camden Mews
London NW1 9AH
England
Tel: +44 171 284 1866
Fax: +44 171 284 1866

Education
BA (Hons) 3D Design,
Manchester Polytechnic,
England, 1992
MA (RCA) Furniture,
Royal College of Art,
London, England, 1994

Collections/commissions
Hat Hill Sculpture Foundation,
permanent collection,
Goodwood Park, Sussex,
England, 1992–94
Private collection,
Sir Terence Conran,
Kintbury, Berkshire, 1994
London Fashion Week
installation, Harvey Nichols,
London, England, 1997

Screen

"S3". Translucent acrylic plastic with stainless-steel pins
and feet.
186 x 172 x 10cm (73.25 x 67.75 x 4in)
In production

"I USE A DIVERSE RANGE OF MATERIALS TO CREATE APPARENTLY SIMPLE OBJECTS, BUT THE UNDERLYING THOUGHT AND DEVELOPMENT IS COMPLEX, REQUIRING INGENUITY AND A DISCIPLINED APPROACH TO RESOLVING CONSTRUCTION AND DETAIL."

08.60 **Andrew Tye**

74 Barnet Grove
Bethnal Green
London E2 7BJ
England
Tel: +44 171 739 3451
Fax: +44 171 739 3451

Education
BA (Hons) 3D Design/
Furniture,
Kingston University,
England, 1990

Collections/commissions
Balustrade for art.tm gallery
commissioned jointly by
art.tm gallery, Inverness,
Scotland, and
The Edward Marshall Trust,
Surrey, England, 1998

Stool and chair
"Polo" stool and chair. Colour-laminated plywood and zinc-plated steel.
44 x seat dia. 28 x base dia. 40cm
(17 x seat 11 x base 15.75in)
In production

08.61 | Juggernaut

David Germond,
Graham Russell,
Steve Jensen and
Geoff Stewart
19–23 Kingsland Road
London E2 8AA
England
Tel: +44 171 739 8070
Fax: +44 171 739 8070

Education
David Germond and Graham
Russell — BA (Hons)
Furniture & Product Design,
Kingston Polytechnic,
England, 1991
Steve Jensen — BA (Hons)
Interior Design,
Kingston Polytechnic,
England, 1991
Geoff Stewart — BA (Hons)
Interior Design,
Middlesex Polytechnic,
England, 1992

Collections/commissions
Cross Bar, Kings Cross,
London, England, 1995
The Zinc Bar, Kilburn,
London, England, 1996
The Highland Gallery
(reception area),
Inverness, Scotland, 1997

Folding table with internal light

"Instantable". Table routed from sheet of translucent polypropylene (in production using CNC routing machine). Fluorescent light attached inside to illuminate table from within. When not in use, table to fold away into its own cardboard storage/carry case.
45 x 60 x 120cm
(17.75 x 23.5 x 47.25in)
Flat-pack 6 x 100 x 100cm
(2.5 x 39.5 x 39.5in)
Prototype

08.62 **Digby Vaughan** 63 Saint Vincent Crescent
Glasgow G3 8NQ
Scotland
Tel: +44 141 204 1582
Fax: +44 141 204 3325

Education
BA (Hons) Furniture Design,
Edinburgh College of Art,
Scotland, 1997

Bench

"Smart Alex" bench seat. Timber seat with cast-aluminium legs.
Available in various timbers, lengths and radii
To commission only

08.63 **Wales & Wales** **Rod and Alison Wales**
Longbarn Workshop
Muddles Green
Chiddingly
Lewes
East Sussex BN8 6HW
England
Tel: +44 1825 872764
Fax: +44 1825 873197

Education
Rod Wales — Designing and
Making in Wood,
Parnham College,
Dorset, England, 1980
Alison Wales — Worked in
John Makepeace's
workshop, 1979-80

Collections/commissions
Cabinet with ten drawers,
Victoria & Albert Museum,
London, England, 1992
Shelf with two drawers,
Shipley Art Gallery,
England, 1994
Concourse and boardroom
furniture for
The Co-operative,
Rochdale, England, 1996

08.64 | **Matt Wingfield** | Unit A 104
Riverside Business Centre
Haldane Place
London SW18 4LZ
England
Tel: +44 181 874 3001
Fax: +44 181 874 3001

Education
BA (Hons) Graphic Design,
Camberwell College of Art,
London, England, 1994
MA (RCA) Printed Textiles,
Royal College of Art,
London, England, 1996

Collections/commissions
Nationwide window display
campaign, Diesel,
London, England, 1997
National window displays,
Ted Baker, eight stores
nationwide, England, 1997
Nationwide window display
campaign (over 66 stores),
Monsoon, England, 1998

Table
Cardboard coffee table. One-piece, flat-pack, silk-screen
printed cardboard table. Hand-printed and machine-cut.
Made up 50.5 x 73.5cm (20 x 29in)
Flat-pack 142 x 96.5cm (56 x 38in)
Prototype being developed for production

1st **Vicky Ghose**

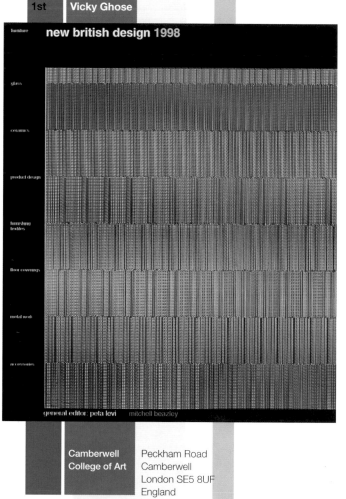

furniture

new british design 1998

glass

ceramics

product design

furnishing
textiles

floor coverings

metal work

accessories

general editor: peta levi   mitchell beazley

**Camberwell
College of Art**

Peckham Road
Camberwell
London SE5 8UF
England

The competition to design the book cover was launched at the beginning of the Spring term, with exceedingly tight deadlines, so we were particularly delighted by the response. 150 designers from 15 colleges participated, with strong submissions from Camberwell College of Art, University of Wolverhampton College of Art & Design, the Royal College of Art and Liverpool John Moores University. The competition was open to second year and final year students and was judged by the book's panel and Gaye Allen, Mitchell Beazley's art director. Allen comments, "the very eclectic mix of design approaches and ideas made the selection process both immensely enjoyable and difficult in equal measure. It seemed particularly apt that ideas for the cover of a book reviewing British design should have such flashes of inventiveness, wit and sheer eccentricity."

The panel had to weigh up an exciting visual approach against a design with an original concept, or choose between something cool and functional and a witty or stylish design. In a very British way the winning design seemed to reflect elements of all of these.

The first prize consists of £250, plus a copy of the book plus £100 worth of Mitchell Beazley books of the winner's choice. The second prize consists of £100 worth of Mitchell Beazley books, and the third prize consists of £50 worth of Mitchell Beazley books.

2nd	Amy Louise Brookes

3rd	Ignacio Espejo

Camberwell College of Art	Peckham Road Camberwell London SE5 8UF England

Liverpool John Moores University	Liverpool Art School 68 Hope Street Liverpool L1 9EB England

Highly Commended

Kim Gehrig

**Central St Martins College
of Art & Design**
School of Graphic and
Industrial Design
Southampton Row
London WC1B 4AP
England

Orla McGrath

**Liverpool John Moores
University**
Liverpool Art School
68 Hope Street
Liverpool L1 9EB
England

Craig France

**Bradford & Ilkley
Community College**
School of Art, Design
and Textiles
Great Horton Road
Bradford BD7 1AY
England

Catherine Sibley

**Camberwell College
of Art**
Peckham Road
Camberwell
London SE5 8UF
England

Retail shops

ENGLAND

LONDON

Aero
96 Westbourne Grove
London W2 5RT
Tel: +44 171 221 1950
Fax: +44 171 221 2555
Wholesale and contract e-mail:
pni@aero-furniture.co.uk
Shop e-mail:
shop@aero-furniture.co.uk
Website: www.areo-furniture.com
Contact: Jonathan McNab
*Contemporary furniture and
accessories available through retail
outlet and catalogue.*

Coexistence
288 Upper Street
London N1 2TZ
Tel: +44 171 354 8817
Fax: +44 171 354 9610
E-mail: coexist1@aol.com
Website: www.coexistence.co.uk
Contact: Mary Wiggin
*Contemporary furniture, lighting and
accessories. Specializes in
packages for the contract market.*

The Conran Shop
Michelin House
81 Fulham Road
London SW3 6RD
Tel: +44 171 589 7401
Fax: +44 171 823 7015
E-mail: conranshop@dial.pipex.com
Website: www.conran.co.uk
Contact: Jeff Heading
*Contemporary and classic designs
for every area and activity in the
home.*

The Conran Shop
55 Marylebone High Street
London W1M 3AE
Tel: +44 171 723 2223
Fax: +44 171 535 3205
E-mail: conranshop@dial.pipex.com
Website: www.conran.co.uk
Contact: Paul Huggins

The Conran Shop Contracts
22 Shad Thames
London SE1 2YU
Tel: +44 171 357 7703
Fax: +44 171 357 7704
E-mail: conranshop@dial.pipex.com
Website: www.conran.co.uk
Contact: Alice Robin
*Works with corporate clients,
architects and designers. Equipped
to furnish hotels, restaurants,
airports, theatres and every type of
office. Bespoke furniture is a
speciality.*

The Furniture Union
46 Beak Street
London W1R 3DA
Tel: +44 171 287 3424
Fax: +44 171 287 3424
Contact: Tanya Roberts
*Contemporary furniture from
established and up-and-coming
designers.*

The Furniture Union
4th Floor
Harvey Nichols
Knightsbridge
London SW1X 7RJ
Tel: +44 171 235 5000
Fax: +44 171 235 6553
Contact: Astrid Barney

Haus
23-25 Mortimer Street
London W1N 7RJ
Tel: +44 171 255 2557
Fax: +44 171 255 1331
E-mail: info@haus.co.uk
Website: www.haus.co.uk
Contact: Michael Mathewson
*Art can be bought in the showroom
and on the internet with pieces from
both new and well-established
artists.*

Heal & Son Limited
196 Tottenham Court Road
London W1P 9LD
Tel: +44 171 636 1666
Fax: +44 171 436 5129
*Large selection of top-quality
contemporary furniture and
accessories for the home. Many
ranges are exclusive and made in
Britain.*

Heal & Son Limited
234 Kings Road
Chelsea
London SW3 5UA
Tel: +44 171 349 8411
Fax: +44 171 349 8439

Liberty plc
Regent Street
London W1R 6AH
Tel: +44 171 734 1234
Fax: +44 171 573 9876
*Famous the world over, Liberty is a
veritable treasure trove of inspiring
and exciting products.*

David Mellor
4 Sloane Square
London SW1W 8EE
Tel: +44 171 730 4259
Fax: +44 171 730 7240
Contact: Dawn Roberts
*David Mellor's original central shop,
selling kitchenware and tableware,
including domestic crafts from
individual practitioners.
Mail-order service available.*

Purves & Purves
80–81 & 83 Tottenham Court Road
London W1P 9HD
Tel: +44 171 580 8223
Fax: +44 171 580 8244
E-mail: mailorder@purves.co.uk
Website: www.purves.co.uk/
Contact: Bill Mailes
*Retailers of contemporary furniture,
lighting and household accessories.*

SCP Limited
135–139 Curtain Road
London EC2A 3BX
Tel: +44 171 739 1869
Fax: +44 171 729 4224
E-mail: scp@scp.co.uk
*A large range of high-quality
residential furniture, from upholstery
to dining tables, lighting and
accessories for the home. SCP
products and furniture from
Cappellini, Driade, B&B and Artek.*

Space
214 Westbourne Grove
London W11 2RH
Tel: +44 171 229 6533
Fax: +44 171 727 0134
Contact: Emma Oldham
*Contemporary furniture and
extraordinary objects, mixing the
more affordable with the limited
edition.*

Themes & Variations
231 Westbourne Grove
London W11 2SE
Tel: +44 171 727 5531
Fax: +44 171 221 6378
Contact: Liliane Fawcett
*Specialists in postwar and modern
contemporary furniture, including
the works of André Dubreuil, Tom
Dixon, Danny Lane and Mark
Brazier-Jones.*

Viaduct Furniture
1–10 Summers Street
London EC1R 5BD
Tel: +44 171 278 8456
Fax: +44 171 278 2844
E-mail: info@viaduct.co.uk
Contact: Catherine Rouxel
*Contemporary British and European
furniture.*

CHIPPING CAMDEN

Robert Welch
The Mill
Lower High Street
Chipping Camden
Gloucestershire GL55 6DS
Tel: +44 1386 840522
Fax: +44 1386 841111
E-mail:
welch@robertwelch.demon.co.uk
Website: www.welch.co.uk
Contact: Rupert Welch
*Contemporary stainless-steel
cutlery, wrought iron, cast iron,
glass, slate and silver household
items.*

GUILDFORD

Heal & Son Limited
Tunsgate
Guildford
Surrey GU1 3QU
Tel: +44 1483 576715
Fax: +44 1483 440 293

LEEDS

The Furniture Union
Harvey Nichols
Victoria Quarter
Briggate
Leeds
West Yorkshire LS1 6AZ
Tel: +44 113 204 8888 ext 5408
Fax: +44 113 204 8889
Contact: Robert Mason

SHEFFIELD

David Mellor Country Shop
The Round Building
Hathersage
Sheffield
South Yorkshire S30 1BA
Tel: +44 1433 650220
Fax: +44 1433 650944
*Kitchenware and tableware,
including domestic crafts from
individual practitioners.*

WARWICK

Robert Welch
19 Old Square
Warwick
Warwickshire CV34 4RU
Tel: +44 1926 400422
Fax: +44 1926 400422
E-mail:
welch@robertwelch.demon.co.uk
Website: www.welch.co.uk
Contact: Rupert Welch

SCOTLAND

EDINBURGH

Inhouse Edinburgh
28 Howe Street
New Town
Edinburgh EH3 6TG
Tel: +44 131 225 2888
Fax: +44 131 220 6632
*Contemporary design, with ranges
of furniture, lighting, rugs, fabrics,
kitchenware and tableware.
Mail-order service available.*

GLASGOW

Inhouse Glasgow
24–26 Wilson Street
Merchant City
Glasgow G1 1SS
Tel: +44 141 552 5902
Fax: +44 141 552 5929
Mail-order service available.

Nice House
The Italian Centre Courtyard
Ingram Street
Glasgow G1 1HD
Tel: +44 141 553 1377
Fax: +44 141 552 5665
E-mail: rad87@dial.pipex.com
Website: www.nice-house.co.uk
Contact: Andrew Harrold
*Contract and retail contemporary
furniture, lighting and accessories
featuring the work of many British
designers.*

OVERSEAS

FUKUOKA

The Conran Shop
Iwataya Z-side 3F
2–5–35 Tenjin
Chou-ku
Fukuoka 810
Japan
Tel: +81 92 726 3717
Fax: +81 92 734 8081

HAMBURG

The Conran Shop
Stilwerk
Große Elbastraße 68
D–22767 Hamburg
Germany
Tel: +49 40 30621 320
Fax: +49 40 30621 333

MELBOURNE

The Conran Shop
Georges
175 Collins Street
Melbourne
Vic 3000
Australia
Tel: +61 3 9929 9999
Fax: +61 3 9654 7604

PARIS

The Conran Shop
117 Rue du Bac
F–75007 Paris
France
Tel: +33 1 42 841 001
Fax: +33 1 42 842 975

TOKYO

The Conran Shop
Living Design Centre: OZONE
Shinjuku Park Tower 3–4F
3–7–1 Nisha-Shinjuku
Shinjuku-ku
Tokyo 163–1062
Japan
Tel: +81 3 5322 6600
Fax: +81 3 5322 6524

Galleries

LONDON

Acadia
87 Charterhouse Street
London EC1M 6JH
Tel: +44 171 490 5533
or +44 171 704 1455
Fax: +44 171 490 5588
Contact: Paul Dean
*Furniture, household and kitchen
objects, including fully bespoke
furniture. A new guest designer will
be featured every six months.*

Barrett Marsden Gallery
17-18 Great Sutton Street
Clerkenwell
London EC1V 0DN
Tel: +44 171 336 6396
Fax: +44 171 336 6391
Contact: Juliana Barrett
*Ceramics, glass, metal, wood,
furniture and mixed media. Regular
solo exhibitions, plus work from
other artists and craftspeople.*

AMSTERDAM

The Frozen Fountain
Prinsengracht 629
1016 HV Amsterdam
The Netherlands
Tel: + 31 20 622 9375
Fax: +31 20 638 3041
Contact: Cok de Rooy
*Specializes in contemporary
furniture, with a strong
representation of work by young
designers, promoted through
permanent but changing collections
and exhibitions.*

Crafts guide

*The following list is an edited
version of the 1998 Crafts Guide,
a register of stockists of quality
crafts in England, Scotland and
Wales, co-ordinated and
produced by Crafts, Britain's
leading decorative and applied
arts magazine. Selection is
undertaken by the Regional Arts
Board or Arts Council responsible
for the region within which a
gallery is located.
The list of outlets included here is
correct at the time of going to
press, but does not comprise the
complete list. A definitive list is
held on the Crafts Council
website at
www.craftscouncil.org.uk*

SCOTTISH ARTS COUNCIL

Roger Billcliffe Fine Art
134 Blythswood Street
Glasgow G2 4EL
Tel: +44 141 332 4027
Fax: +44 141 332 6573
*Monthly applied arts exhibitions on
three floors, from leading makers in
ceramics, glass, metalwork,
jewellery, textiles and automata.
Commissioning service.*

Broughton Gallery
Broughton Place
Broughton
near Biggar
Strathclyde ML12 6HJ
Tel: +44 1899 830234
*British crafts, paintings and original
prints. Exhibition programme
available by post. Commissioning
service.*

Open Eye Gallery
75-79 Cumberland Street
Edinburgh EH3 6RD
Tel: +44 131 557 1020
Fax: +44 131 557 1020
25 contemporary crafts exhibitions held throughout the year, specializing in ceramics, wood, glass, jewellery and sculpture, along with changing stock displays. Commissioning service.

The Scottish Gallery
16 Dundas Street
Edinburgh EH3 6HZ
Tel: +44 131 558 1200
Fax: +44 131 558 3900
E-mail: mail@scottish-gallery.co.uk
The Scottish Gallery has mounted over 100 exhibitions of contemporary British and occasionally European crafts, with a specific emphasis on ceramics, jewellery, metalwork, glass and wood. Commissioning service.

The Strathearn Gallery & Pottery
32 West High Street
Crieff
Tayside PH7 4DL
Tel: +44 1764 656100
E-mail: info@strathearn-gallery.com
The gallery exhibits a large selection of art and crafts. Regular exhibitions are held throughout the year. A working pottery is located in the gallery basement. Commissioning service.

NORTHERN ARTS

Clayton Gallery
14 Clayton Road
Jesmond
Tyne & Wear NE2 4RP
Tel: +44 191 281 2560
Fax: +44 191 281 6734
E-mail: clayton-gallery@onyxnet.co.uk
Changing exhibitions of British crafts alongside a programme of contemporary art.

Cleveland Crafts Centre
57 Gilkes Street
Middlesbrough
Cleveland TS1 5EL
Tel: +44 1642 262376
Fax: +44 1642 226351
The centre's shop represents established makers alongside newcomers and local craftspeople. Commissioning service.

Earth Works
9a Narrowgate
Alnwick
Northumberland NE66 1JH
Tel: +44 1665 606300
Craft work in a range of disciplines. Commissioning service.

Northern Gallery for Contemporary Art
City Library and Arts Centre
Fawcett Street
Sunderland
Tyne & Wear SR1 1RE
Tel: +44 191 514 1235
Fax: +44 191 514 8444
E-mail: ngca@sund2.unity.libris.co.uk
The craft shop stocks a wide range of jewellery, glass, ceramics, toys, textiles, wood and metal works, lights, clocks and handmade cards, along with contemporary art and craft magazines, catalogues and library publications. Commissioning service.

Old Court House Gallery
Market Place
Ambleside
Cumbria LA22 9BU
Tel: +44 1539 432022
Fax: +44 1539 433022
E-mail: gallery@oldcourtgallery.demon.co.uk
Comprehensive range of contemporary ceramics, glass, metal, wood, jewellery and mixed media. Commissioning service.

Portcullis
7 The Arcade
Metro Centre
Gateshead
Tyne & Wear NE11 7YL
Tel: +44 191 460 6345
Fax: +44 191 460 4285
E-mail: tic@portcullis.demon.co.uk
Designer crafts, with an emphasis on precious and non-precious jewellery, glass, ceramics, textiles, wood and metal. Commissioning service.

Williamson Brown
20a Clayton Road
Jesmond
Tyne & Wear NE2 4RP
Tel: +44 191 281 8273
Fax: +44 191 281 8287
Work from silver and goldsmiths from around the country, together with collections from jewellers Kirkham and Turner, who design and make on the premises. Commissioning service.

YORKSHIRE & HUMBERSIDE ARTS

The Craft Centre and Design Gallery
Leeds City Art Gallery
The Headrow
Leeds
West Yorkshire LS1 3AB
Tel: +44 113 247 8241
Specializes in a large display of contemporary crafts, plus domestic and studio ceramics, textiles, glass, wood and a large selection of limited-edition fine-art prints. Exhibitions, showcases and promotions held throughout the year.

Design House Gallery
Dean Clough
Halifax
West Yorkshire HX3 5AX
Tel: +44 1422 250250
Fax: +44 1422 255250
E-mail: linda@design.dimension.co.uk
Contemporary furniture, lighting, textiles, ceramics, jewellery and accessories by British designers and makers. Only permanent venue for work by members of New Designers in Business. Commissioning service.

European Ceramics
The Warehouse
Finkle Street
Knaresborough
North Yorkshire HG5 8AA
Tel: +44 1423 867401
Fax: +44 1423 867401

Robert Feather Jewellery Gallery
10 Gillygate
York
North Yorkshire YO3 7EQ
Tel: +44 1904 632025
Specializing mainly in contemporary jewellery, plus a selection of other crafts.

Godfrey and Twatt
7 Westminster Arcade
Parliament Street
Harrogate
North Yorkshire HG1 2RN
Tel: +44 1423 525300
A wide selection of contemporary crafts and original prints regularly in stock. Four exhibitions held a year.

Pyramid
43 Stonegate
York
North Yorkshire YO1 2AW
Tel: +44 1904 641187
A broad selection of contemporary British crafts, specializing in jewellery and ceramics.

NORTH WEST ARTS

The Arc
4 Commonhall Streeet
Chester
Cheshire CH1 2BJ
Tel: +44 1244 348379
Fax: +44 1244 348379
A wide range of quality crafts. Varied exhibition programme. Commissioning service.

Artizana
The Village
Prestbury
Cheshire SK10 4DG
Tel: +44 1625 827582
Fax: +44 1625 827582
Two sections house contemporary work by British makers, one specializing in furniture, the other featuring jewellery, ceramics, wood, and glass. Commissioning service.

Bluecoat Display Centre
Bluecoat Chambers
School Lane
Liverpool L1 3BX
Tel: +44 151 709 4014
Fax: c/o +44 151 707 0048
E-mail: crafts@bluecoat.u-net.com
A range of British contemporary crafts: studio pottery, ceramics, wood, glass, jewellery, textiles and metal work. Commissioning service.

The Craft Centre
Royal Exchange Theatre
Heron House
Albert Square
Manchester M2 5I ID
Tel: +44 161 833 9333
Fax: +44 161 832 0881
Temporarily housed, returning in November 1998. Contemporary crafts including jewellery, ceramics, glass, wood. Exhibition programme restarting when relocated. Commissioning service.

EAST MIDLANDS ARTS

Ashbourne Gallery
50 St John Street
Ashbourne
Derbyshire DE6 1DT
Tel: +44 1335 346742
Fax: +44 1335 347101
An eclectic mix of work. Commissioning service.

Castle Museum Craft Shop
Castle Museum
Nottingham
Nottinghamshire NG1 6EL
Tel: +44 1159 153662
Fax: +44 1159 153 653
Ranges of work by contemporary makers specializing in jewellery, ceramics and glass.

The City Gallery
90 Granby Street
Leicester
LE1 1DJ
Tel: +44 1162 540 595
Fax: +44 1162 540 593
The shop displays a changing collection of crafts for sale, while the craft gallery hosts themed or specialized exhibitions. Commissioning service.

Ferrers Centre for Arts & Crafts
Ferrers Gallery
Staunton Harold
Ashby-de-la-Zouch
Leicestershire LE6 5RW
Tel: +44 1332 863337
Fax: +44 1332 865408
Wide range of work. Regular exhibitions. Commissioning service.

Magpie Gallery
2 High Street West
Uppingham
Rutland LE15 9QD
Tel: +44 1572 822212
Changing selections of contemporary crafts by new and established makers.

Rufford Craft Centre
Rufford Country Park
near Ollerton
Newark
Nottinghamshire NG22 0DF
Tel: +44 1623 822944
Fax: +44 1623 824702
E-mail: rufford@btinternet.com
Website: www.ruffordcraftcentre.org.uk
The gallery maintains a varied programme of major craft exhibitions. Commissioning service.

Derek Topp Gallery
Chatsworth Road
Rowsley
Matlock
Derbyshire DE4 2EH
Tel: +44 1629 735580
E-mail: derektoppgallery@btinternet.com
Independent contemporary applied arts gallery exhibiting the work of more than 60 British artists. Commissioning service.

EASTERN ARTS

Cambridge Contemporary Art
6 Trinity Street
Cambridge
CB2 1SU
Tel: +44 1223 324222
Fax: +44 1223 315606
E-mail: cam.cont.art@dial.pipex.com
Displays and exhibitions of contemporary crafts. Commissioning service.

Craft at the Castle
Norwich Castle Museum
Castle Meadow
Norwich
Norfolk NR1 3JU
Tel: +44 1603 493628
Fax: +44 1603 765651
Local and national craft makers feature in an ever-changing shop selection.

Craft Co.
40a High Street
Southwold
Suffolk IP18 6JA
Tel: +44 1502 723211
A co-operative shop offering a selection of handmade contemporary crafts, mainly by local makers. Commissioning service.

The Gowan Gallery
3 Bell Street
Sawbridgeworth
Hertfordshire CM21 9AR
Tel: +44 1279 600004
Fax: +44 1279 832494
Continually changing varied display of contemporary craft work. Precious jewellery made at the gallery workshop by Jane Gowan. Commissioning service.

The Pearoom Centre for Contemporary Crafts
Station Yard
Station Road
Heckington
Lincolnshire NG34 9JJ
Tel: +44 1529 460765
Fax: +44 1529 460948
Two galleries with an ongoing programme of contemporary craft exhibitions, workspace for five resident craftspeople, and retail shop. Annual programme of short courses. Commissioning service.

Primavera
10 Kings Parade
Cambridge
CB2 1SL
Tel: +44 1223 357708
A wide selection of contemporary work held in stock, alongside changing solo and mixed exhibitions throughout the year.

Pam Schomberg Gallery
12 St John's Street
Colchester
Essex CO2 7AN
Tel: +44 1206 769458
Shop and gallery exhibiting and selling a range of contemporary craftwork. Commissioning service.

Lynne Strover Gallery
23 High Street
Fen Ditton
Cambridgeshire CB5 8ST
Tel: +44 1223 295264
Regular exhibitions of leading sculptural and studio ceramics: Baldwin, Jupp, Welch. Commissioning service.

Torkington Gallery
38 St Peters Street
Stamford
Lincolnshire PE9 2PF
Tel: +44 1780 762281
Studio ceramics by makers from East Anglia and the Midlands. Ceramics, jewellery and hand-painted silks are produced at the gallery. Commissioning service.

Unit 2 Gallery
The Rural Workshops
Station Road
Docking
Norfolk PE31 8LT
Tel: +44 1485 518817
Shop and gallery exhibiting and selling a range of contemporary craftwork.

Workshop Design
3 Bridge Street
Cambridge
CB2 1UA
Tel: +44 1223 354326
Fax: +44 1223 354326
Fine jewellery, studio glass and leather goods by UK-based craftsmen and women. Own jewellery workshop on the premises. Commissioning service.

ARTS COUNCIL OF WALES

Aberystwyth Arts Centre
University of Wales
Penglais
Aberystwyth
Dyfed SY23 3DE
Tel: +44 1970 622887
or +44 1970 622895
Fax: +44 1970 622883
The shop stocks works from leading makers as well as holding regular craft shows, together with ceramic series exhibitions featuring the work of a particular maker.

Brook Street Pottery
Brook Street
Hay-on-Wye
Herefordshire HR3 5BQ
Tel: +44 1497 821026
Fax: +44 1497 821063
Specializing in contemporary tableware. Also sells and makes a range of terracotta garden ware, and holds three or four exhibitions a year, including textiles, metalwork, jewellery and other crafts. Commissioning service.

Countryworks Gallery
Broad Street
Montgomery
Powys SY15 6PH
Tel: +44 1686 668866
Contemporary craftwork and paintings.

The Golden Sheaf Gallery
25 High Street
Narberth
Pembrokeshire SA67 7AR
Tel: +44 1834 860407
Fax: +44 1834 869064
Comprehensive selection of contemporary crafts and art. Commissioning service.

Meridian Contemporary Arts
13 High Town
Hay-on-Wye
Herefordshire HR3 5AE
Tel: +44 1497 821633
Fax:+44 1497 821633
Contemporary fine and applied art. Commissioning service.

Model House Craft & Design Centre
Bull Ring
Llantrisant
Rhondda Cynon Taff
Mid Glamorgan CF72 8EB
Tel: +44 1443 237758
Fax: +44 1443 224718
Offers a programme of contemporary craft exhibitions and a comprehensive range of contemporary British crafts.

Oriel Mostyn
12 Vaughan Street
Llandudno
Gwynedd LL30 1AB
Tel: +44 1492 879201
Fax: +44 1492 878869
Craftwork from all over Britain, including jewellery, textiles, wood, ceramics and glass. Commissioning service.

Oriel Myrddin
Church Lane
Carmarthen
Dyfed SA31 1LH
Tel: +44 1267 222775
A changing display of contemporary designer crafts sits alongside exhibitions of craft/design and fine art from leading makers and artists throughout the UK, plus associated education and activities programmes.

Porticus
1 Middleton Street
Llandrindod Wells
Powys LD1 5ET
Tel: +44 1597 823989
Stocks a wide range of work by British makers and new designers. The gallery has a diverse exhibition programme. Commissioning service.

Ruthin Craft Centre
The Gallery
Park Road
Ruthin
Clwyd LL15 1BB
Tel: +44 1824 704774
Fax: +44 1824 702060
Contemporary applied art from across Britain, with a wide-ranging exhibition programme.

West Wales Arts Centre
16 West Street
Fishguard
Dyfed SA65 9AE
Tel: +44 1348 873867
Fax: +44 1348 873867
Specializes in contemporary ceramics from both international and newly-established makers. Lecture programme and facilities available. Commissioning service for jewellery and silversmithing.

WEST MIDLANDS ARTS

Anderson Gallery
96 High Street
Broadway
Worcestershire WR12 7AJ
Tel: +44 1386 858086
Fax: +44 1386 858086
A varied stock of crafts and paintings. Commissioning service.

Artifex
Hungry Horse Craft Centre
Weeford Road
Sutton Coldfield
Birmingham B75 6NA
Tel: +44 121 323 3776
Fax: +44 121 323 3776
As well as a permanent collection of work, Artifex also has a showroom devoted to fine contemporary furniture. Commissioning service.

Collection Gallery
The Southend
Ledbury
Herefordshire HR8 2EY
Tel: +44 1531 634641
Fax: +44 1531 631555
Three or four large themed exhibitions a year, calendar available. Commissioning service.

The Kilvert Gallery
Ashbrook House
Clyro
Herefordshire HR3 5RZ
Tel: +44 1497 820831
Fax: +44 1497 820831
A contemporary art gallery with a wide range of designer objects and crafts. Commissioning service.

Lion Gallery
Lion House
15b Broad Street
Leominster
Herefordshire HR6 8BT
Tel: +44 1568 611898
Website: www.cogent-comms.co.uk/lion.htm
Specializing in work produced mainly in North Herefordshire and the Borders. Commissioning service.

Montpellier Gallery
8 Chapel Street
Stratford-upon-Avon
Warwickshire CV37 3EP
Tel: +44 1789 261161
Fax: +44 1789 261161
British crafts including studio ceramics, glass, wood and designer jewellery. Also exhibiting sculpture, contemporary painting, printmaking. Commissioning service.

Old Chapel Gallery
East Street
Pembridge
near Leominster
Herefordshire HR6 9HB
Tel: +44 1544 388842
Fax: +44 1544 388842
Wide range of contemporary crafts on permanent display. Exhibitions held regularly throughout the year. Commissioning service.

Ombersley Gallery
Church Terrace
Ombersley
Worcestershire WR9 0EP
Tel: +44 1905 620655
Fax: +44 1905 620655
Regular exhibitions, both solo and mixed. Permanent display of work. Occasional talks and events arranged in connection with exhibitions. Commissioning service.

Round House Gallery
38 High Street
Tutbury
near Burton upon Trent
Staffordshire DE13 9LS
Tel: +44 1283 814964
Established and emerging ceramics and jewellery. Regular exhibitions. Relocating to Faston in late 1998.

Shire Hall Gallery
Market Square
Stafford S116 2LD
Tel: +44 1785 278345
Fax: +44 1785 278327
British crafts from new and established makers.

Three Pears Gallery
17 Friar Street
Worcester WR1 2NA
Tel: +44 1905 619333
Fax: +44 1905 619333
Wide range of contemporary arts. Promotes local and new artisans, with regular themed and one-person exhibitions in upstairs gallery. Commissioning service.

SOUTH WEST ARTS

Alpha House Gallery
South Street
Sherborne
Dorset DT9 3LU
Tel: +44 1935 814944
Fax: +44 1935 814617
Regular exhibitions of work by established and young artists and craftspeople, principally in ceramics, sculpture and painting. Permanent stock of new ceramics by leading potters.

Beaux Arts
12-13 York Street
Abbey Square
Bath
Avon BA1 1NG
Tel: +44 1225 464850
Fax: +44 1225 422256
Specialists in modern 20th-century painting, sculpture and modern British ceramics. Regular solo exhibitions by well-known and up-and-coming artists. Commissioning service.

Black Swan Guild
2 Bridge Street
Frome
Somerset BA11 1BB
Tel: +44 1373 473980
Shop selling contemporary crafts, with changing monthly exhibitions in ceramics, textiles and jewellery. Gallery space with exhibitions of contemporary art and craft throughout the year. Commissioning service.

Brewery Arts
Cirencester Workshops Trust
Brewery Court
Cirencester
Gloucestershire GL7 1JH
Tel: +44 1285 657181
Fax: +44 1285 644060
Contemporary craft shop within a unique arts centre, comprising a large shop, exhibition gallery, theatre, 16 resident craftworkers, education studios and sculpture school. Commissioning service.

Church House Designs
Broad Street
Congresbury
Bristol
Avon BS19 5DG
Tel: +44 1934 833660
British contemporary crafts, with particular emphasis on ceramics and glassware. Exhibitions at least twice yearly. Commissioning service.

Cowdy Gallery
31 Culver Street
Newent
Gloucestershire GL18 1DB
Tel: +44 1531 821173
A specialist gallery selling studio glass by designer-makers. Exhibitions reflect current developments in art glass. Commissioning service.

Dansel Gallery
Rodden Row
Abbotsbury
near Weymouth
Dorset DT3 4JL
Tel: +44 1305 871515
Fax: +44 1305 871518
E-mail: dansel@wdi.co.uk/dansel
Website: www.wdi.co.ul/dansel
Specializes in contemporary woodwork, including one-off bowls, boxes, desk accessories, domestic ware, clocks, furniture and toys. Commissioning service.

Dartington Cider Press Centre
Shinners Bridge
Dartington
Totnes
Devon TQ9 6TQ
Tel: +44 1803 864171
Fax: +44 1803 866094
A wide range of contemporary crafts from national and international makers.

Devon Guild of Craftsmen
Riverside Mill
Bovey Tracey
Devon TQ13 9AF
Tel: +44 1626 832223
Fax: +44 1626 834220
E-mail: francis-byng@crafts.org.uk
A wide range of work from the South-West region, with a programme of one-person and themed exhibitions by national makers. Commissioning service.

Simon Drew Gallery
13 Foss Street
Dartmouth
Devon TQ6 9DR
Tel: +44 1803 832832
Fax: +44 1803 833040
Functional, decorative and sculptural ceramics in stoneware, porcelain and earthenware on permanent display. Commissioning service.

Juliet Gould Gallery
1 Church Street
Mevagissey
Cornwall PL26 6SP
Tel: +44 1726 844844
Craft work includes some of Britain's leading potters shown alongside contemporary paintings by artists from the West Country. Monthly seasonal exhibitions. Commissioning service.

Higher Street Gallery
"The Shambles"
1 Higher Street
Dartmouth
Devon TQ6 9RB
Tel: +44 1803 833157
Contemporary work, sculpture, paintings and etchings. Commissioning service.

Hitchcocks
10 Chapel Row
off Queen's Square
Bath
Avon BA1 LHN
Tel: +44 1225 330646
Fax: +44 1225 330646
Specializing in mechanical toys and textiles from Britain and Ireland. Commissioning service.

Mid-Cornwall Galleries
St Blazey Gate
Par
near St Austell
Cornwall PL24 2EG
Tel: +44 1726 812131
Exhibits a wide range of fine contemporary work from British makers and artists. Nine exhibitions a year.

New Craftsman
24 Fore Street
St Ives
Cornwall TR26 1HE
Tel: +44 1736 795652
Specializes in a wide variety of crafts by leading British makers. Also shows paintings, sculpture and prints by artists working in Cornwall. Commissioning service.

St James's Gallery
9b Margarets Buildings
Bath
Avon BA1 2LP
Tel: +44 1225 319197
Exhibits a wide range of contemporary ceramics, jewellery, paintings and prints. Commissioning service.

Six Chapel Row
6 Chapel Row
off Queen's Square
Bath
Avon BA1 1HN
Tel: +44 1225 337900
Fax: +44 1225 336577
Gallery shows contemporary fine and applied art in a programme of monthly exhibitions by artists and craftspeople from UK and overseas. Commissioning service.

Studio Pottery
West Country Ceramics
15 Magdalen Road
Exeter
Devon EX2 4TA
Tel: +44 1392 430082
Fax: +44 1392 430082
E-mail:
studio.pottery@mail.inxpress.co.uk
Website:
www.inxpress.co.uk/studio.pottery
*Open by appointment only.
Specialist ceramics gallery showing
work by leading potters. Publisher of
Studio Pottery magazine.*

Traffords
Digbeth Street
Stow-on-the-Wold
Gloucestershire GL54 1BN
Tel: +44 1451 830424
*Wide range of British contemporary
crafts. Commissioning service.*

Walford Mill Craft Centre
Stone Lane
Wimborne Minster
Dorset BH21 1NL
Tel: +44 1202 841400
*Contemporary crafts shop, ground-
floor exhibition gallery, workshops
and education centre.
Commissioning service.*

Yew Tree Gallery
Steanbridge Lane
Slad
near Stroud
Gloucestershire GL6 7QE
Tel: +44 1452 813601
*A variety of contemporary British
craft and paintings. Commissioning
service.*

SOUTHERN ARTS

Artworks
7 The Shambles
Bradford-on-Avon
Wiltshire BA15 1JS
Tel: +44 1225 863532
*Specializes in contemporary crafts,
featuring the work of new designer-
makers, together with those more
established. Commissioning service.*

Bay Tree Gallery
26 West Street
Alresford
near Winchester
Hampshire SO24 9AT
Tel: +44 1962 735888
Fax: +44 1428 727303
*An extensive range of contemporary
ceramics, glass, silver and metals.
Commissioning service.*

**Beatrice Royal Contemporary
Art and Craft Gallery**
Nightingale Avenue
Eastleigh
Hampshire SO50 9JJ
Tel: +44 1703 610592
Fax: +44 1703 610596
*The largest selling contemporary art
and craft gallery in the south of
England. Commissioning service.*

Bettles Gallery
80 Christchurch Road
Ringwood
Hampshire BH25 5NG
Tel: +44 1425 470410
Fax: +44 1425 479002
*Holds a comprehensive stock of
ceramics by leading British makers
and also features eight or nine solo
or group exhibitions annually.
Commissioning service.*

Candover Gallery
22 West Street
Alresford
near Winchester
Hampshire SO24 9AE
Tel: +44 1962 733200
*Established since 1984.
Commissioning service.*

Eton Applied Arts
81 High Street
Eton
Windsor
Berkshire SL4 6AF
Tel: +44 1753 860771
Fax: +44 1753 622292
E-mail: etonarts@bogo.co.uk
*Displays innovative work by British
makers. Commissioning service.*

Fenny Lodge Gallery
Simpson Road
Bletchley
Milton Keynes
Buckinghamshire MK1 1BD
Tel: +44 1908 642207
Fax: +44 1908 647840
*An extensive range of ceramics,
glass and jewellery. Commissioning
service.*

**Fisherton Mill Design and
Contemporary Craft Emporium**
108 Fisherton Street
Salisbury
Wiltshire SP2 7QY
Tel: +44 1722 415121
Fax: +44 1722 415121
*British contemporary crafts and
design. Commissioning service.*

New Art Centre
Roche Court Sculpture Park
East Winterslow
near Salisbury
Wiltshire SP5 1BG
Tel: +44 1980 862244
Fax: +44 1980 862447
*Shows ceramic pots, wood and
brick furniture and sculpture in many
other media. Commissioning
service.*

Oxford Gallery
23 High Street
Oxford OX1 4AH
Tel: +44 1865 242731
Fax: +44 1865 242731
*Contemporary applied arts.
Commissioning service.*

Sea Street Crafts
Quay Arts Centre
Sea Street
Newport Harbour
Isle of Wight PO30 5BD
Tel: +44 1983 822490
Fax: +44 1983 649606
*Craft display area creates a regional
centre for arts and crafts.
Commissioning service.*

Waterfront Museum
4 High Street
Poole
Dorset BH15 1BW
Tel: +44 1202 683138
Fax: +44 1202 660896
*Work by locally and nationally
known makers across a wide range.
Displays are often linked to the
museum exhibitions programme.*

We Three Kings
19 Bridge Street
Witney
Oxfordshire OX8 6DA
Tel: +44 1993 775399
Fax: +44 1993 775399
*A selection of work including
jewellery, ceramics, glass and wood,
and a resident goldsmith working at
the bench within the gallery.
Commissioning service.*

LONDON ARTS BOARD

Amalgam
3 Barnes High Street
London SW13 9LB
Tel: +44 181 878 1279
*Specialists in ceramic container
forms by new and established
makers. Also blown glass, jewellery
and prints.*

Galerie Besson
15 Royal Arcade
28 Old Bond Street
London W1X 3HB
Tel: +44 171 491 1706
Fax: +44 171 495 3203
*Permanent stock of classic potters –
Coper, Rie, Leach, Cardew,
Henderson, Fritsch, Lee and others
– potters from Denmark, Russia,
Spain and Japan. Monthly
exhibitions.*

Cecilia Colman Gallery
67 St John's Wood High Street
London NW8 7NL
Tel: +44 171 722 0686
*Wide selection of British ceramics,
glass and jewellery. Also mirrors and
carved wood. Regular exhibitions.*

Contemporary Applied Arts
2 Percy Street
London W1P 9FA
Tel: +44 171 436 2344
*Membership association with
regular exhibitions and a shop.
Posting, packaging and overseas
shipping can be arranged.
Commissioning service.*

Contemporary Ceramics
William Blake House
7 Marshall Street
London W1V 1LP
Tel: +44 171 437 7605
Fax: +44 171 287 9954
*Retail outlet for the Crafts Potters
Association. Large selection of
ceramics, from mugs to sculptural
pieces.*

Crafts Council Gallery Shop
44a Pentonville Road
London N1 9BY
Tel: +44 171 806 2559
Fax: +44 171 837 6891
E-mail: admin@craftscouncil.org.uk
Website: www.craftscouncil.org.uk
*All work selected by the Crafts
Council, mainly to compliment the
exhibition programme. Stocks a
wide range of crafts publications,
which are also available by mail
order. Commissioning service.*

Crafts Council Shop at the V&A
Victoria & Albert Museum
South Kensington
London SW7 2RL
Tel: +44 171 581 0614
Fax: +44 171 837 6891
*All work selected from members of
the Crafts Council Index, Crafts
Council grant recipients and makers
represented in the Crafts Council
Collection.*

Lesley Craze Galleries
33-35 Clerkenwell Green
London EC1R 0DU
Tel: +44 171 608 0393
or +44 171 251 9200
*Extensive collection of precious
jewellery and mixed media, including
pieces from designers working in
non-precious materials. Also
contemporary textiles, selling work
by around 60 textile designers and
fibre artists.*

Fitch's Ark
6 Clifton Road
London W9 1SS
Tel: +44 171 266 0202
Fax: +44 171 266 0060
*Animal imagery — birds, beasts,
sea creatures — in various
contemporary crafts. Regular
exhibitions of new and established
artists.*

Frivoli
7a Devonshire Road
London W4 2EU
Tel: +44 181 742 3255
Fax: +44 181 994 7372
*Selection of top makers and new
talent.*

The Glasshouse
21-22 St. Albans Place
Islington
London N1 0NX
Tel: +44 171 359 8162
Fax: +44 171 359 9485
*Studio glass workshop/gallery
featuring pieces by Annette Meech,
Christopher Williams, David Taylor
and Fleur Tookey.*

SOUTH EAST ARTS

The Bank Gallery
73-75 High Street
Chobham
Surrey GU24 8AF
Tel: +44 1276 857369
Fax: +44 1276 857369
*The gallery houses the work of
British designer-makers. Regular
exhibitions in the main gallery and
the new textile room.
Commissioning service.*

Hugo Barclay
7 East Street
Brighton
East Sussex BN1 1HP
Tel: +44 1273 321694
Fax: +44 1273 725959
E-mail: hugo@hugobarclay.co.uk
Website: www.hugobarclay.co.uk
*Individual work by UK makers. More
than 120 artists are represented
annually. Regular exhibitions.*

Charleston
Firle
near Lewes
East Sussex BN8 6LL
Tel: +44 1323 811626
Fax: +44 1323 811628
*The Charleston Shop sells
distinctive art by contemporary
makers working in the tradition of
the Charleston artists — ceramics,
textiles, jewellery and painted
furniture.*

Fire and Iron Gallery
Rowhurst Forge
Oxshott Road
Leatherhead
Surrey KT22 0EN
Tel: +44 1372 386453
Fax: +44 1372 386516
*Centre for the exhibiting, retailing
and commissioning of British and
international decorative metalwork.
Blacksmithing demonstrations,
courses and special exhibitions
supplement an extensive permanent
display. Commissioning service.*

Furniture 151
151 High Street
Lewes
East Sussex BN7 1XU
Tel: +44 1273 488443
Fax: +44 1273 488442
*Batch-produced craftwork.
Commissioning service.*

The Gibbs Gallery
53 Palace Street
Canterbury
Kent CT1 2DY
Tel: +44 1227 763863
*Stocks the work of leading British
craftspeople and jewellers, with four
major exhibitions each year.
Commissioning service.*

**The Grace Barrand Design
Centre**
19 High Street
Nutfield
Surrey RH1 4HH
Tel: +44 1737 822865
Fax: +44 1737 822617
*Shop, gallery and mews studio
where day schools and short
courses are held. Commissioning
service.*

New Ashgate Gallery
Wagon Yard
Lower Church Lane
Downing Street
Farnham
Surrey GU9 7PS
Tel: +44 1252 713208
Fax: +44 1252 737398
*Changing exhibitions of two- and
three-dimensional work, giving equal
emphasis to established and
promising new artists and makers.
Craft gallery and jewellery studio.
Commissioning service.*

Paddon & Paddon
113 South Street
Eastbourne
East Sussex BN21 4LU
Tel: +44 1323 411887
*A diverse range of crafts by leading
contemporary makers, with around
80 individual craftspeople
represented. Summer and Autumn
exhibitions are held annually.
Commissioning service.*

Hannah Peschar Gallery
Black & White Cottage
Standon Lane
Ockley
Surrey RH5 5QR
Tel: +44 1306 627269
Fax: +44 1306 627662
*Sculpture and ceramics.
Commissioning service.*

Index

Index by name

Acknowledgements

I would like to thank the selection panel – Jane Priestman, James Park and Michael Marriott – for all their hard work and good humour over the selection process; also Emmanuel Cooper, editor of *Ceramic Review*, and Cyril Frankel, the ceramics expert, and his team in Bonhams Futures Department for their advice.

I very much appreciate the commitment and enormous help given by Stephen Masterson, Christine Wallace, Sarah Brooks, and Freya Burton.

Peta Levi

Mitchell Beazley and Peta Levi are extremely grateful for the the cooperation of all the designers in helping to put this book together in a very short space of time. Inevitably, due to time pressures there have been some omissions of deserving designers. Next year we hope to include those we missed due to restrictions of space and time. We welcome submissions for next year's edition.

Picture Acknowledgements
Ceramics: 13 (top right) **Neil Mersh,** 21 **Bill Osment,** 32 **Stephen Brayne.**
Glass: 46/7 **John Holford-Clamp,** 51 **Heaney and Mill Studios.**
Lighting: 65 **Richard Davies,** 87 (both pictures) **Christine Sullivan.**
Furnishing Textiles: 122, 155 (bottom right) **Abbas Nazari.**
Metalwork: 174 **Simon Phillips.**
Furniture: 212 **Richard Davies,** 214 (bottom left) **Forty Four,** 217 (bottom left) **Frank Thurston,** 229 **John Holford-Clamp,** 231 (top) **Julian Hawkins,** 236 **Graham Pearson,** 239 (bottom right) **David Churchill/Arcaid,** 257 (both pictures) **Steve Speller.**